MEMORY GAMES
FOR SENIORS

This Book
Belongs To

_____

_____

Contents

Introduction

Thank you for picking up this book! Whether you're looking to sharpen your memory, keep your brain active, or just enjoy some relaxing activities, you've come to the right place.

This book is filled with carefully designed brain exercises, logic puzzles, and memory games that are not only fun but also help boost your cognitive skills. All the activities in this book are large print and easy to read, making them perfect for anyone looking for a gentle yet engaging mental challenge.

Remember, there's no rush—go at your own pace, and most importantly, have fun! Whether you're completing a crossword, solving a maze, or finding hidden words, each page is here to entertain and sharpen your mind.

So grab a pencil, relax, and let's get started on this exciting journey to keep your brain active and healthy!

Happy puzzling!

Memory Games

Select the image from 1-6 that matches the top view of the 3D object.

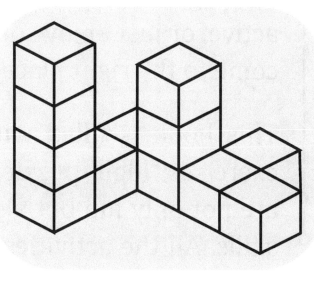

1

2

3

4

5

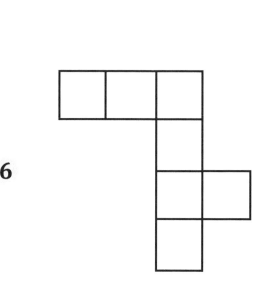

6

MEMORY LISTS

Study the tables of words and images below for 1 minute. The words and images are numbered identically. When you're ready, turn to the next page and answer the memory questions. Try not to peek back!

Banana	Chair	Dog	Newspaper	Apple
Book	Car	Phone	Pen	Glasses
Lamp	Table	Pillow	Shoes	Clock

Now, answer the following questions based on what you remember from the lists of words and images on the previous page. Try to complete the questions from memory without looking back!

What was the word in position 6? _____

What was the image in position 8? _____

Which word was in position 10? _____

Name two images that represent something found outside.

_____

Name three words from the table that are objects you can wear.

_____

What image was in position 12? _____

Which image shows something that can cut things?

_____

What word was in position 3? _____

Which two words describe items used in a living room?

_____

What was the word in position 15? _____

How many images in total represent objects you might take on a trip?

_____

What was the image in position 5? _____ 6

FIND TWO IDENTICAL SHAPES

Look carefully at the shapes in each square. Your task is to find the two squares that contain exactly the same shape.

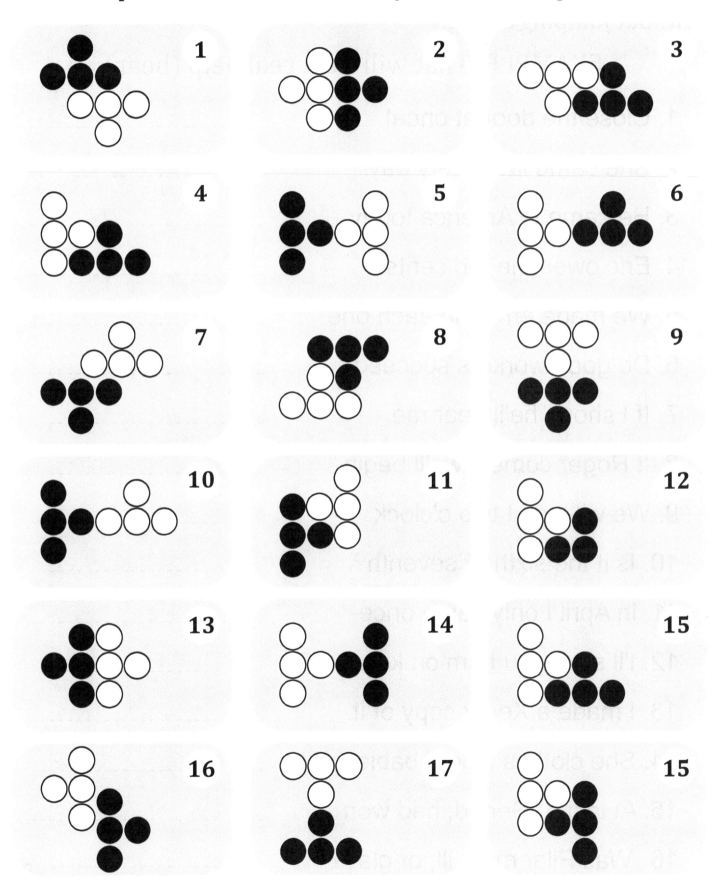

Find the hidden animal in each sentence below. The animal's name may be spread across multiple words. Try to spot them without jumping ahead!

EXAMPLE: That will **be a r**eal help (bear)

1. Close the door at once! _____

2. She came late every day. _____

3. He came to America today. _____

4. Eric owes me ten cents. _____

5. We made errors in each one. _____

6. Do good workers succeed? _____

7. If I shout, he'll hear me. _____

8. If Roger comes, we'll begin. _____

9. We will go at two o'clock. _____

10. Is it the sixth or seventh? _____

11. In April I only came once. _____

12. I'll sing; you hum on key. _____

13. I made a Xerox copy of it. _____

14. She clothes naked babies. _____

15. At last, I, Gerald, had won _____

16. Was Pilar mad, ill, or glad? _____

SPOT THE DIFFERENCE

Study both pictures carefully and find the 8 differences between them

9

WHAT'S THE WORD?

Use the clues and the given hints to figure out the mystery word in each level. Each level increases in difficulty, so take your time and think carefully.

Level 1: Easy

1. Furry Pet   H _ _ _ _ _ _

2. Yellow Fruit   B _ _ _ _ _

3. School Subject   S _ _ _ _ _ _

4. Large Body of Water   O _ _ _ _

5. Opposite of Fast   S _ _ _

Level 2: Getting Tricky

6. U.S. State   _ _ _ _ F _ _ _ _ _

7. Famous Wizard   _ _ _ B _ _ _ _ _ _

8. Type of Tree   _ _ K

9. Musical Instrument   _ I _ _ _ _

10. Winter Sport   _ _ _ _ _ _ W _ _ _ _ _ _ _

Level 3: Insanely Tough

11. Element on the Periodic Table   _ _ _ R _ _ _ _

12. Famous Painting   _ _ _ _ L _ _ _

13. Precious Gem   S _ _ _ H _ _ _

14. Type of Dinosaur   _ _ _ _ _ _ _ P _

15. Famous Landmark   _ _ F _ _ _   _ _ _ _ _

REMEMBER THE DETAILS

Take a moment to memorize the picture below. When you're ready, turn the page to find an identical picture that is missing 3 details

FIND IT

Look at the section provided and find where it fits in the grid below. There's only one correct place for it. Can you spot the exact location?

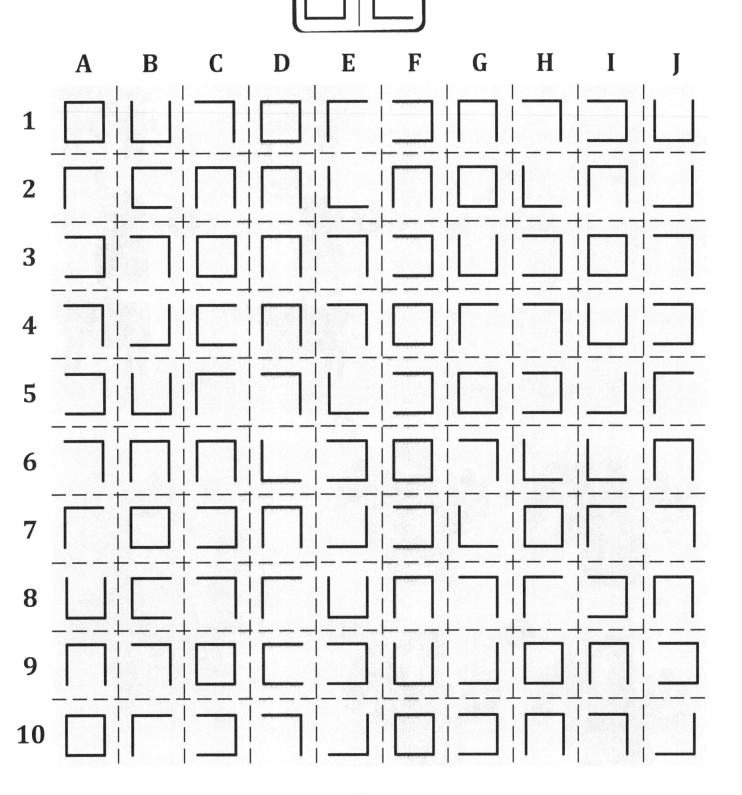

Can you find the correct Shadow?

WORD WALL

Study the words below for 2 minutes. Then turn the page to answer questions from memory. Try not to look back!

Strawberry	Computer	Basketball	Pillow	Easter
Halloween	Flower	Guitar	Chair	Banana
Table	Bicycle	Boat	Watermelon	Valentine's Day
Oven	Clock	Cat	Airplane	Popcorn
Candle	Elephant	Football	Sandwich	Sunglasses

Turn The Page

15

WORD WALL – QUESTIONS

1. How many fruits were on the wall? _____

2. Can you name all the fruits? _____

3. Which holidays were on the wall? _____

4. What word was in the middle of the second row?

_____

5. What forms of transportation were on the wall?

_____

6. Can you name all the items you might find in a house?

_____

7. What word was in the top left corner? _____

8. What musical instrument was on the wall? _____

9. What word was directly below "Pillow"? _____

10. In the third column, can you recall the first three
    words?

_____

11. What word was above "boat"? _____

12. What was the last word in the second column? _____

13. What word was in the bottom right corner? _____

14. What word was in the top right corner? _____

15. Can you name the sports mentioned? _____

16

SQUARES

Look at the six squares below, each containing a different pattern of colored sections. Study the shapes for 1 minute. When you're ready, turn the page and try to recreate the same patterns from memory. Try not to look back!

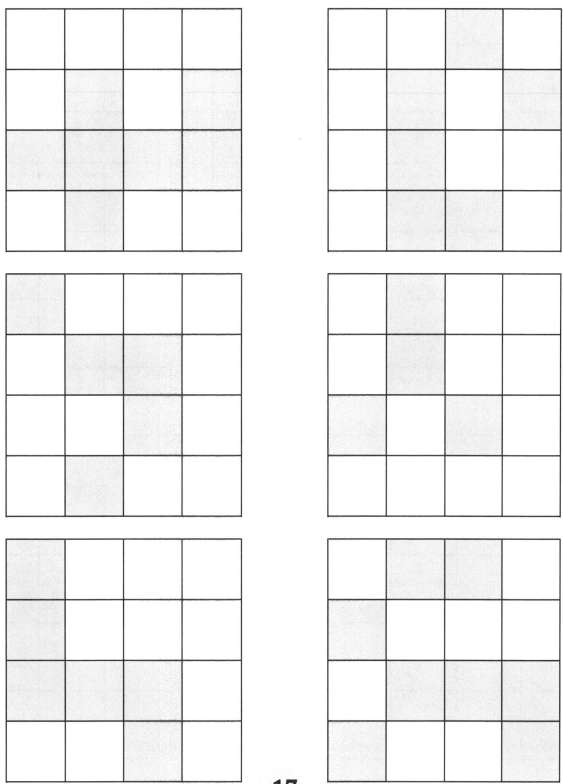

Study both pictures carefully and find the 8 differences between them

Crossword Puzzles

CROSSWORD #1

Across

2. U.S. State
6. Note of reference below text at bottom of page
7. Japanese form of self-defense
8. Greek god of love
10. Eskimo dwelling
12. Golf mounds
13. Baking chamber
14. To cut and harvest crops

Down

1. Unruly crowd
3. Land measure
4. Speech delivered by one actor
5. Jamaican popular music
9. Took a seat
10. Monetary unit of Peru
11. Suitable for traveling over rough terrain

CROSSWORD #2

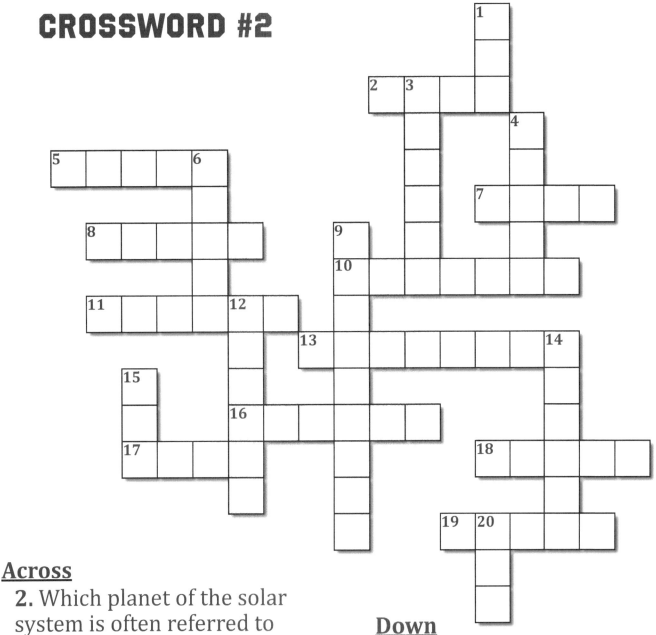

Across

2. Which planet of the solar system is often referred to as the red planet

5. Capital of Morocco

7. Remain

8. What celestial object, when near the sun, has a tail which points away from the sun

10. Prolonged period of dryness

11. Enrages

13. Consisting of metal

16. Abrading tool

17. Space agency

18. The unit of frequency

19. Restraint to control animal

Down

1. Distress signal

3. What do astronomers call the proportion of incident light that is reflected by the surface of a planet or moon

4. Game played with pet

6. At that place

9. Describes or modifies a noun

12. 40th president of the U.S

14. Group of singers

15. Brown shade

20. Self-esteem

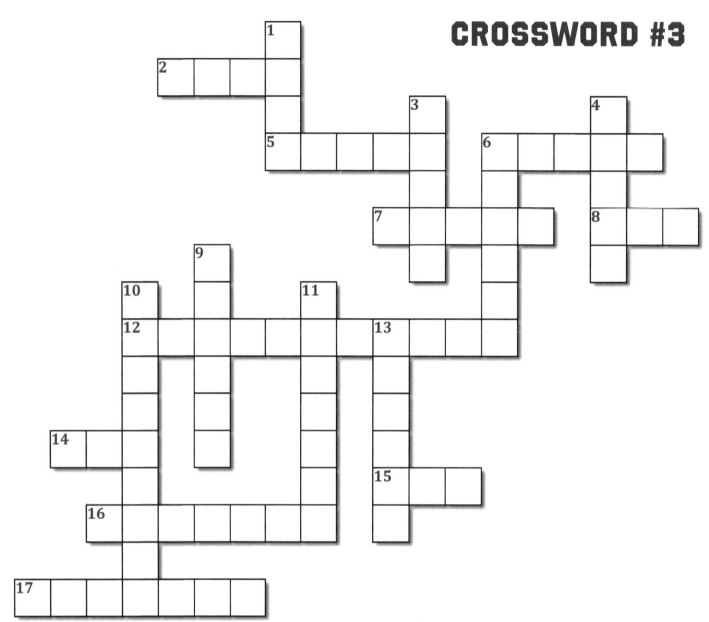

Across

2. Official language of Pakistan
5. Small lizard
6. Horse race
7. Four-door car
8. Clumsy person
12. Science of growing crops
14. Nocturnal bird
15. Electrically charged atom
16. Manipulating soil for growing crops
17. Tower on church

Down

1. Manure
3. Fictitious narrative
4. Monastery head
6. Capable of being done
9. Window on a sloping roof
10. Man-made orbiter
11. The why and wherefore
13. Strategic maneuver

CROSSWORD #4

23

Across

1. First woman
3. Spray painting tool
5. Serving plate
6. Former coin of Spain
7. My, French (Plural)
10. Stories
12. Worships
14. Female sheep
15. Otic organ
16. Short often comical piece

Down

1. Developer of the theory of relativity
2. Washed out
4. Instrument for measuring atmospheric pressure
8. Monetary unit of Iran
9. Work is measured in this unit
10. Small or large rocks floating in space
11. Prolonged unconsciousness
13. Uproar

Across

2. Reflected sound
4. Army rank
7. Detachment
8. Military organization that conducts war on the sea
11. Amphibian
12. Capital of Madagascar
13. August birth flower
16. Actor in minor, non-speaking role
17. Borders

Down

1. Ear part
2. A Great Lake
3. Monetary unit of Western Samoa
5. Release of emotional tension
6. Egyptian beetle
9. Image of a deity
10. Laugh loudly
14. What is the unit of electrical current
15. Fresh-water fish

CROSSWORD #6

Across
3. Point of attention
6. Agitate
8. Tall, tapered tower
9. Pet form of Leonard
11. Bird of prey
12. Bright explosion of a star
15. Serve as the subject of a verb
16. Something to aim for
17. 12 constellations

Down
1. Elaborately carved grotesque architectural feature
2. Sprite of Irish folklore
3. Torment pet and owners
4. Club porter
5. Capital of Virginia
7. Faucet
10. Military vehicle with four-wheel drive
13. Male deer
14. Small role played by famous actor

CROSSWORD #7

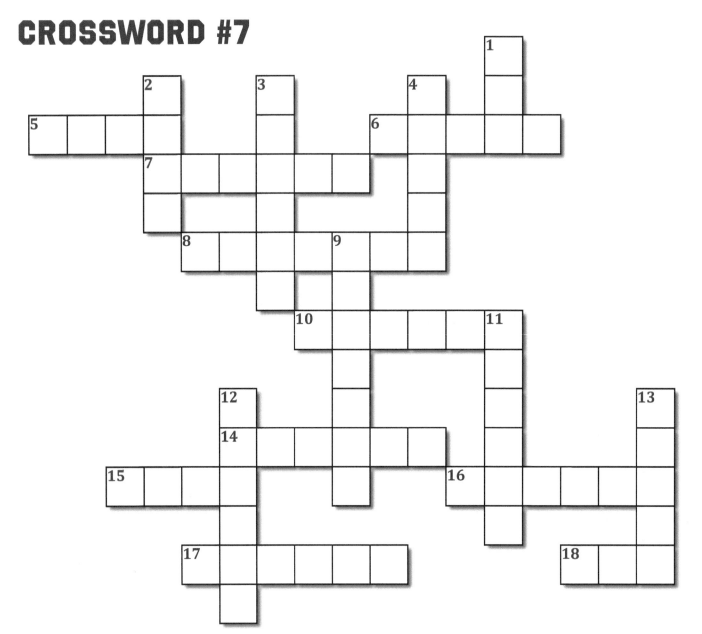

Across

5. Exploding star
6. Seeped
7. Stomach (Childish) (3-3)
8. Small bomb that is thrown by hand
10. Grins
14. Large lizard
15. Device to ensnare
16. Avoids
17. Cure
18. Commercials

Down

1. - kwon do (Korean martial art)
2. Western pact
3. More moist
4. Body of deputised hunters
9. Commander of a fleet of ships
11. Unhealthy
12. Crab's claw
13. Electrical safety devices

Across

3. Fencing sword

5. Tall-growing grain

6. Distort

11. Adverse reaction

12. Vast number of celestial bodies

13. Ancient Hebrew coin

16. Small slender long-tailed parrot

17. Compass point

18. Hitler's autobiography, '-Kampf'

Down

1. Musical drama

2. Spun by spiders

4. Upward current of warm air

7. Bottomless gulf

8. Chief god of ancient Greece

9. Explodes a bomb

10. To calculate or predict

14. Old stringed instruments

15. Adventurous expedition

CROSSWORD #9

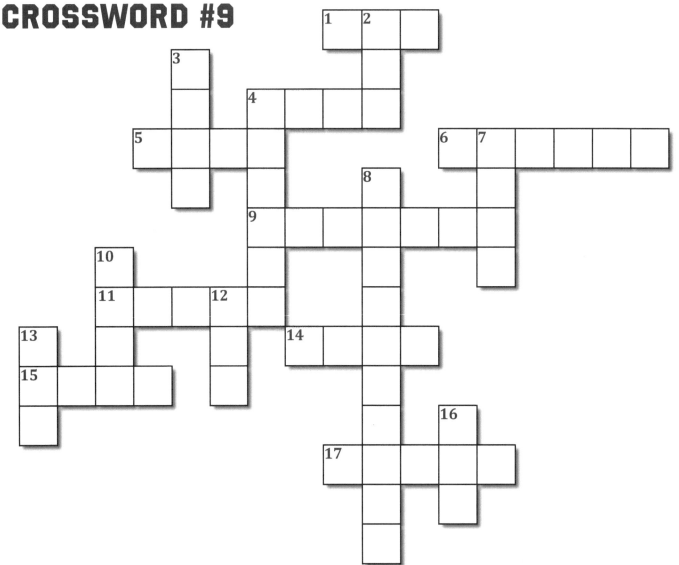

Across

1. Large van

4. Sounds of disapproval

5. Type of cheese

6. Come out of a surrounding environment

9. Act of withdrawing from a place

11. Slender pointed shaft shot from a bow

14. First letter of the Arabic alphabet

15. Acquired Immune Deficiency Syndrome (abbr.)

17. Feudal superior

Down

2. Ship initials

3. Lacking heat

4. Tunnel dug by certain animals

7. Story of traditional knowledge of a society

8. Act of foretelling

10. Greeting _____

12. Tree

13. Period between sunrise and sunset

16. Stage of life

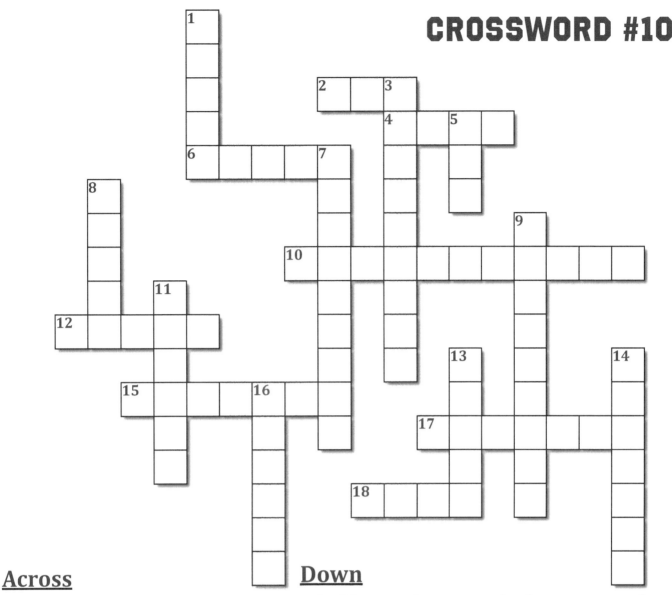

Across

2. Prisoner of War

4. Occurrence believed to be supernatural

6. Rough or unpleasant

10. Hell

12. Small boat with pointed ends that is moved by using a paddle

15. August birth stone

17. Military group that fights on land and sea

18. Take a long walk in the country for fun

Down

1. Place where cattle, horses, or sheep are raised

3. Groundhog

5. Greek goddess of the dawn

7. Remain dormant over winter in a den

8. Black and white Chinese animal

9. Land mass higher than a hill

11. Small four-footed mammal with sharp teeth

13. Visual representation

14. Pastime of catching or trying to catch a fish

16. Dry sandy area with few plants

Logic Puzzles

DOUBLE AND TRIPLE!

Can you figure it out? Give it a try!

Place the numbers 1, 2, 3, 4, 6, 7, 8, and 9 to form three different three-digit numbers in such a way that:

• The number in the second row is equal to double the number in the first row.

• The number in the third row is equal to double the number in the second row.

	8	

CHANGE TWELVE LETTERS

Start with the revealed word. Solve each clue by changing one letter of the previous word to form a new word. Continue around the circle until you return to the starting word. Good luck!

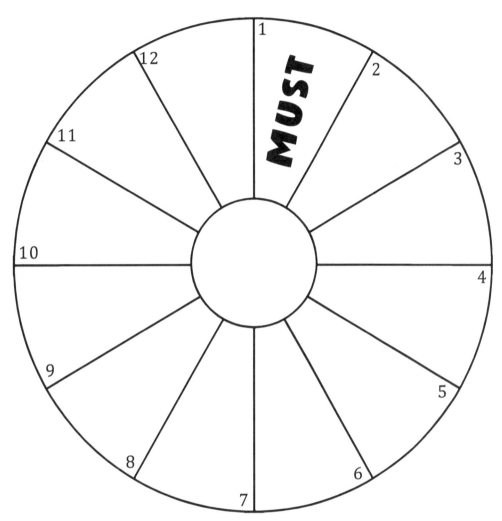

2. Fog, low cloud

3. It holds the sail on a ship

4. Not the future

5. Send a letter or parcel

6. You don't know where you are

7. Coming after all the others

8. Write things in order, perhaps with numbers

9. Old fashioned word meaning "for fear that, so that"

10. Put your feet up, take a breather

11. Red crust on old metal

12. Broke, broken

THE RACE AND FAVORITE TV SHOWS

Use the clues below to match each runner to their finishing time, the TV show they watched, and the house they live in. Fill in the grid to solve the puzzle.

		First Names				Tv Shows				Houses			
		Ben	Emma	Sam	Chloe	Wild Adventures	Planet Earth	Mystery Hour	The Comedy Club	Modern House	Farmhouse	Cottage	Villa
Times	2 min, 59 sec												
	3 min, 2 sec												
	3 min, 5 sec												
	3 min, 8 sec												
Houses	Wild Adventures												
	Planet Earth												
	Mystery Hour												
	The Comedy Club												
Tv Shows	Modern House												
	Farmhouse												
	Cottage												
	Villa												

Clues:

1. Sam didn't watch Wild Adventures or Planet Earth.
2. The owner of the Modern House is Chloe.
3. The runner who finished with a time of 3 min, 2 sec watched The Comedy Club.
4. Of the owner of the Farmhouse and Sam, one completed the race at 2 min, 59 sec and the other completed the race at 3 min, 5 sec.
5. The person who watched Mystery Hour finished after the person who watched Planet Earth.
6. The owner of the Villa is not Emma and didn't watch Mystery Hour.
7. Either the owner of the Farmhouse or the owner of the Cottage watched Planet Earth.
8. Ben doesn't live in the Farmhouse and didn't watch The Comedy Club.
9. Emma finished before Sam.

Times	First Names	Tv Shows	Houses
2 min, 59 sec			
3 min, 2 sec			
3 min, 5 sec			
3 min, 8 sec			

Find the correct three-digit combination using the clues from the unsuccessful attempts.

To open the safe, you need to figure out the three-digit code. Here are some attempts made by someone who didn't succeed:

- 1 2 3   None of the numbers are correct.

- 4 5 6   One number is correct and in the right place.

- 6 1 2   One number is correct but in the wrong place.

- 5 4 7   One number is correct but in the wrong place.

- 8 4 9   One number is correct and in the right place.

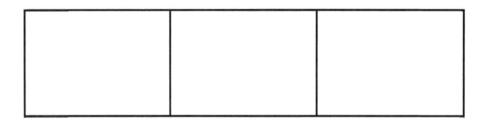

UNINTERRUPTED PATH

Place the numbers from 1 to 36 in the grid to create an uninterrupted path. The numbers must connect either horizontally, vertically, or diagonally, without any breaks.

	42	1				
	40	49	4	5		8
	48		36		9	
	47	37		35		
	46	29	31			13
		23		19	14	
					18	

1. Move three matchsticks to make two squares.

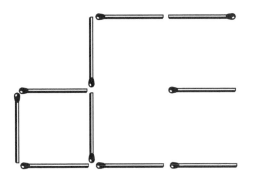

4. Move two matchsticks to make four squares.

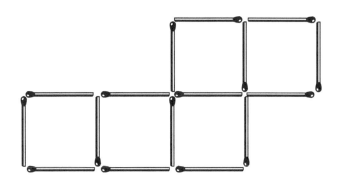

2. Move three matchsticks to make two squares.

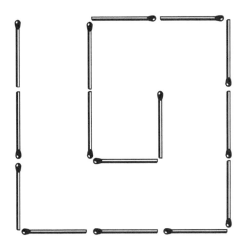

5. Move four matchsticks to make three squares.

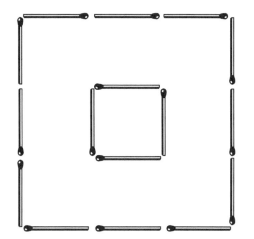

3. Move three matchsticks to make three squares.

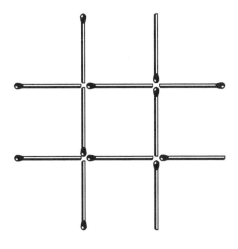

6. Move three matchsticks to make four squares.

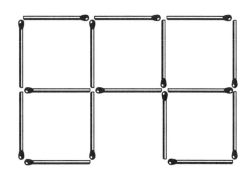

THE LASER BEAM PUZZLE

We want to deflect the laser beam using mirrors like the ones shown below:

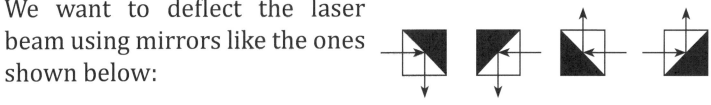

The laser can burst balloons when it passes through them:

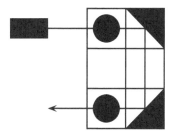

Place exactly 6 mirrors on the grid below to make the laser burst all the balloons.

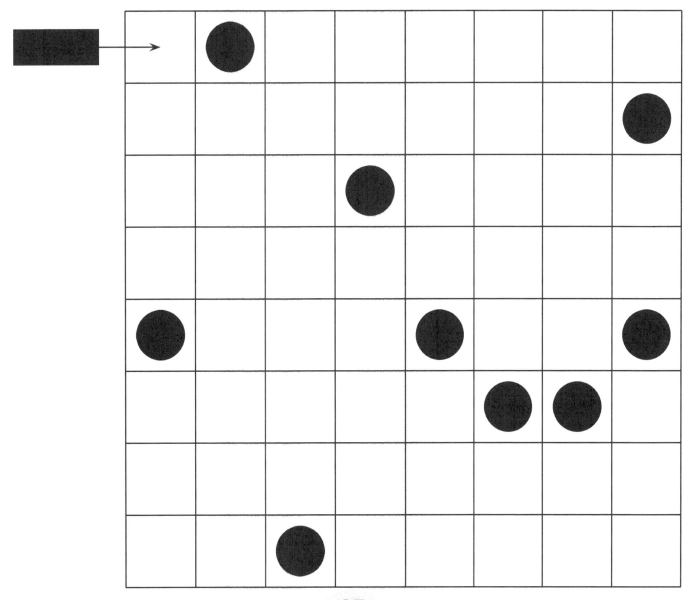

TEA TIME LOGIC PUZZLE

Use the clues to figure out each employee's name, last day of work, hobby, and favorite tea. Mark the correct answers on the chart and eliminate the rest to complete the puzzle. Each person has a unique combination of these details.

		First Names					Hobbies					Teas				
		Angelo	Avery	Damian	Elijah	Jayden	astronomy	bicycling	painting	reading	skydiving	black tea	green tea	herbal tea	oolong tea	white tea
Last Day Of Work	January 31															
	February 19															
	June 12															
	October 23															
	December 9															
Teas	black tea															
	green tea															
	herbal tea															
	oolong tea															
	white tea															
Hobbies	astronomy															
	bicycling															
	painting															
	reading															
	skydiving															

Clues:

1. The person who enjoys bicycling is Damian.
2. Either the person who drank black tea or the person who drank green tea enjoys painting.
3. The person who drank green tea does not enjoy painting.
4. The 5 people were the person who drank herbal tea, the person who enjoys reading, the employee whose last day will be December 9, Angelo, and the person who drank black tea.
5. Avery will leave before the person who enjoys reading.
6. The person who drank oolong tea does not enjoy astronomy.
7. Of Jayden and Elijah, one is leaving the company on October 23 and The employee whose last day will be January 31 drank black tea.
8. The person who drank herbal tea will leave after the person who enjoys astronomy.
9. The employee whose last day will be June 12 didn't drink white tea.
10. Elijah will leave before the person who drank herbal tea.

Last Day Of Work	First Names	Hobbies	Teas
January 31			
February 19			
June 12			
October 23			
December 9			

THE TRIANGULAR GARDEN

In the triangular garden below, four plant pots are already lined up. Your task is to place six more pots to create five lines, each containing four pots.

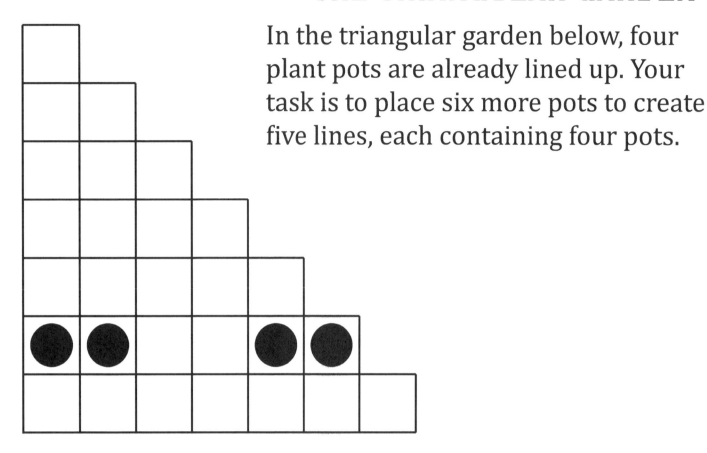

THE GUARDIANS

Place five guardians (pawns) on the chessboard. Each guardian controls its row, column, and diagonal, eliminating any tokens found in those directions.

Can you arrange the guests Correctly around the table?

Scenario:

Around a round table, Roger is immediately to the left of Sam. Lily is neither next to Emma nor immediately to the right of John, but she is across from Rachel. There are only six people at the table.

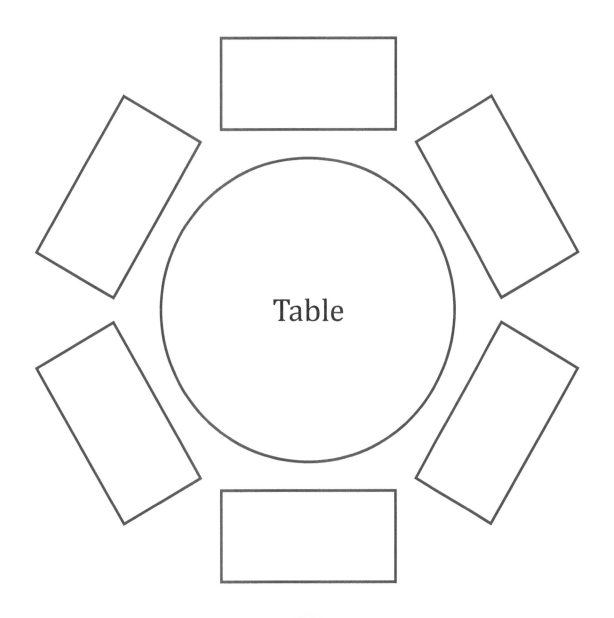

Word Searches

Find the hidden words in the puzzle. Each word can appear horizontally, vertically, or diagonally. Take your time and enjoy the search.

GARDENING

```
T M A H M M J X S W J C A J Q P W J
N P M R Q X G W Y E S O A C I C P C
R R E L T Y V Y T T L M U L T O M D
Z R D I Z P J C P S H R U B F M T L
N I Q I S R L L U T O H O E P Z I
S S M L Q U W A T E R I N G R O P T
N H Y X L N T W N B F E L R T S S P
P I O Z H I C N I T D O O E I T R H
K N I V K N B R T R V K M E L U R N
A O P M E G K F A R D O A N I J H P
B S S U N L I G H T O J U H Z M W W
A D X U I E F F N L V O U O E T Z E
G V X Y B H L R B Q X J T U R R L E
Q X D X G R R W H Y K R T S T E B D
S J K G W J J A D M R O S E S E C S
```

Rose	Shovel	Sunlight	Weeds
Tulip	Plant	Garden	Shrub
Watering	Fertilizer	Pruning	Bloom
Greenhouse	Tree	Lawn	Roots
Hoe	Compost	Herbs	Soil

TRAVEL DESTINATIONS

```
M I Z Y T V E N I C E W X O B E R H
C A I R O K S E W B T I H Z G O N V
G D D Q I K Y W W L D R L D Y L Z E
T W T R F E D Y U E D U O E I L C X
B E R L I N N O U W B K B B C N V E
P K K O I D E R H N B E K A E N T V
C O N R M S Y K A K U O A R I S V L
C F Z C D E B T V G K V O C D A J M
U A T H E N S O A G F L V E M Z U V
Y I B P S I J R N Z F L J L B Q Q W
U I S C J T P A A F C S O O B U H K
S A Z Q H B B A N X O B Y N J U V K
W Z T C E M D O R E B K D A D M S U
R D X O T F A I A I O T U O C O Z G
G J H N J J D Z Y T S P U G D W N X
```

Paris	New York	Dubai	Seoul
Rome	Cairo	Bangkok	Istanbul
Tokyo	Berlin	Venice	Lisbon
London	Madrid	Barcelona	Prague
Sydney	Athens	Florence	Havana

```
F Q C P W Q K E Y Z N K U Z Q H X V
Y C D R P O L L O C K Q E J E T L E
P V E W G M I D U V Y R R B T I Z R
N U T Z J Z M N K R B E M U T U C M
O A A U W V T I G A P N R M Y V L E
B I T D R A H X C P Q O E O F V S E
I V F T E N R E O H V I M N F S A R
E G A O J G E H J A E R B E I C M K
P T U S D O X R O E X L R T G Y E P
B V C C W G F D A L I G A D A Z O I
A X K F V H G T P L M M N N U Z J C
C A R A V A G G I O A V D N G B L A
A Q S H V G Z U M A N E T J U E Y S
C J U I F K O L D A V I N C I M L S
F O Z L J I M L E C E Z A N N E S O
```

Da Vinci	Michelangelo	Raphael	Turner
Picasso	Dali	Caravaggio	Klimt
Van Gogh	Warhol	Vermeer	Pollock
Monet	Renoir	Cezanne	Hopper
Rembrandt	Matisse	Gauguin	Manet

```
X  K  J  X  T  L  P  E  L  I  C  A  N  C  N  S  C  X
J  I  W  Y  C  D  F  P  E  A  C  O  C  K  H  P  A  E
A  W  O  O  D  P  E  C  K  E  R  N  U  A  U  A  R  N
P  O  A  N  O  P  P  I  G  E  O  N  F  V  M  R  D  Q
C  V  E  T  V  S  D  S  H  C  B  C  Y  R  M  R  I  P
J  Q  D  Y  E  D  E  W  L  C  I  H  E  G  I  O  N  B
Y  V  X  L  H  C  H  A  H  W  N  I  J  B  N  W  A  E
F  G  W  V  C  O  F  L  G  L  E  C  E  U  G  A  L  E
N  O  R  D  R  R  W  L  W  U  O  U  M  M  B  S  J  I
E  W  V  F  A  K  O  O  K  W  L  Q  W  U  I  C  J  G
F  K  W  C  N  E  I  W  N  B  D  L  B  L  R  A  U  I
I  T  D  G  E  P  A  R  R  O  T  S  V  J  D  P  A  V
A  K  B  P  E  H  H  G  M  Y  F  B  D  I  M  S  Z  M
D  Z  P  I  X  D  B  M  L  W  Q  T  J  E  Z  T  T  G
J  J  M  B  S  I  V  P  N  E  U  T  E  A  H  K  G  G
```

Eagle	Robin	Parrot	Peacock
Sparrow	Falcon	Crow	Pelican
Owl	Heron	Bluebird	Swallow
Woodpecker	Hawk	Seagull	Dove
Pigeon	Crane	Cardinal	Hummingbird

COOKING INGREDIENTS

```
N Q I Z H Z L W E K Z H Y G S Q B C
N P N D K R P E U A V P B R W N D Y
N C I N N A M O N L K B X Q E B R Q
T M T P X Y E D J K L U G K I A L D
J G R K H N Y R Q I G C C T M D E B
K V I T O M A T O P D I M E M Y T A
Q Q B S P G W E N L H F S V E G G S
G K N R U K V B I C D O J I N D D I
Z N K S A I F L O U R R N N R M S L
T I A U L R U W N P E P P E R N J T
P P R O X B F A W T I P G G Y M A T
E F P J I Y G G T Q P N Z A V O K K
P Q Q E B I O U U M I L K R I C E W
F C U M N R B W F G A R L I C T P W
P B K O O C N Y Z S A L T S B N U P
```

Flour	Tomato	Oliveoil	Cinnamon
Sugar	Chicken	Vinegar	Ginger
Butter	Basil	Rice	Honey
Garlic	Salt	Milk	Thyme
Onion	Pepper	Eggs	Rosemary

```
I Z B I I M K F R D O S N G M E Y R
H W I Z A R D O F O Z T Y L S M M I
J W V X J I C W V D C W U A L I E N
P E G U W I K Q J M X K E D E N S D
M S X F N L J R E B U R Y I F D O I
E T Y A O R J D N B G R A A L G U A
R S T C U H P U L P F I C T I O N N
J I I H H X V E R T I G O S D D A
T D N G H O S T B U S T E R S F O J
Q E C H G O O D F E L L A S H A F O
B S V W T Y Z L S P M W Z Q S T M N
U T J Q Q C F W N G R D H U W H U E
S O W C A S A B L A N C A F O E S S
X R D M A J B T T M K H K P J R I S
X Y F O R R E S T G U M P P S K C T
```

Casablanca	Star Wars	Gladiator	Ben-Hur
Vertigo	Godfather	Wizard of Oz	West Side Story
Psycho	Rocky	Alien	Sound of Music
Titanic	Forrest Gump	Ghostbusters	Goodfellas
Jaws	Indiana Jones	Grease	Pulp Fiction

```
B Q A Y P I U M G Z D X M L D D U R
O O S R M W Y I B Q R J T T E U J O
N B H L M W E N K T E V O D W B Z W
H N A H K R P U V H P C L Y V A X L
E R K R X Z R Z D S Y I K R C L I I
P H E P T C B J T P W N I O L E B N
R H S Y C H A N A U S T E N G L I G
Q E P Z Z R V T W E C O N R A D N S
D M E L V I L L E C V O O P Y I E H
B I A H E S C F G O R W E L L C L E
J N R F I T Z G E R A L D P G K I L
K G E Q G I Q G A P Z P I P O E O L
M W M S T E I N B E C K B R O N T E
I A V Q H U A E E Q N R A W L S S Y
W Y U V L A F Z J P J O C Q D O C F
```

Shakespeare	Fitzgerald	Christie	Conrad
Dickens	Twain	Steinbeck	Shelley
Hemingway	Tolkien	Bronte	Kipling
Austen	Poe	Melville	Eliot
Orwell	Rowling	Joyce	Wilde

OUTDOOR ACTIVITIES

```
C T E C U Y P F B S A I L I N G T E
N G V F A E O I S U A G M W M O Y T
K Y Z V L M C S X R G O Y G O L B H
L N V X H O P H C F G X N S O F E Z
D N E T E N N I S I G I K L X I D C
A T W S Y U P N N G R G G N S A
W R K D N H H G I G M L P N O G Y N
W M A M F O L F O S R L I Y K C E O
M Q Y Y G S R J R B W K W D R X R E
V A A F U X K A S I I W A T S U I
V W K Z S H O G E H Q K M N C K N N
E S I D W E O K A L C L I M B I N G
F S N O W B O A R D I N G N I I I A
O I G V O L G A R D E N I N G N N X
W B I R D W A T C H I N G A A G G M
```

Hiking	Kayaking	Running	Jogging
Camping	Swimming	Surfing	Sailing
Fishing	Climbing	Snowboarding	Golfing
Canoeing	Birdwatching	Tennis	Snorkeling
Biking	Skiing	Gardening	Windsurfing

```
P  Y  R  A  M  I  D  S  S  J  G  P  M  C  F  R  W  S
X  U  A  B  M  T  U  Y  T  U  R  M  L  O  D  G  X  T
E  U  C  I  O  C  D  D  P  O  A  I  M  L  L  G  M  A
F  L  R  G  U  G  P  N  X  M  N  V  A  O  E  O  O  T
F  E  O  B  N  G  G  E  R  B  D  E  C  S  A  L  U  U
B  I  P  E  T  R  A  Y  O  U  C  B  H  S  N  D  N  E
G  F  O  N  R  E  T  O  K  R  A  W  U  E  I  E  T  O
F  F  L  R  U  A  P  P  R  J  N  Q  P  U  N  N  E  F
X  E  I  G  S  T  N  E  E  K  Y  J  I  M  G  G  V  L
A  L  S  K  H  W  I  R  M  H  O  I  C  X  T  A  E  I
Q  T  A  J  M  A  H  A  L  A  N  O  C  U  O  T  R  B
C  O  A  K  O  L  A  Y  I  L  B  Y  H  L  W  E  E  E
Z  W  N  O  R  L  D  K  N  I  X  B  U  A  E  E  S  R
I  E  O  L  E  N  Y  K  Y  F  X  X  P  N  R  D  T  T
N  R  H  Q  C  N  I  A  G  A  R  A  F  A  L  L  S  Y
```

Eiffel Tower	Machu Picchu	Statue of Liberty	Niagara Falls
Great Wall	Stonehenge	Pyramids	Sydney Opera
Taj Mahal	Petra	Leaning Tower	Grand Canyon
Big Ben	Kremlin	Golden Gate	Mount Everest
Colosseum	Mount Rushmore	Acropolis	Burj Khalifa

```
N P G H L T O V I O L I N C U R H I
F P E U Z R R I Q E P R I B E A A B
Q D L P I A N O N E T Z G H M O R I
L A P J X T W L M I R M X C W V P T
N Q L J K R A A B B M N Q O H D E P
Q Y C I O Y H R S K O I J F D P A H
X L E L V R F L U T E N J P M T B O
R Y Q C A N G X X U A U E U N V X J
H G L D I R T A M B O U R I N E G J
A C C O R D I O N A A T I N P J M M
I M L B P U Z N M F D S X X F O X Z
V U B K X H M C E L L O S W N H U S
B C Y L A B O S D T R C E O I Q C V
X H H A R M O N I C A H S A O L B R
S A X O P H O N E L G O N M F N M P
```

Guitar	Flute	Banjo	Organ
Piano	Drums	Trombone	Tuba
Violin	Saxophone	Accordion	Viola
Cello	Clarinet	Tambourine	Bassoon
Trumpet	Harp	Xylophone	Harmonica

Roundabouts

WHAT IS A ROUNDABOUT PUZZLE?

The Roundabouts puzzle is a grid of squares. Some squares have circles, which are called "roundabouts."

To solve the puzzle, draw a path that goes through the center of every square, making sure the path doesn't cross over itself. The path should eventually come back to where it started.

When the path reaches a roundabout, it must turn. Between any two roundabouts, the path must change direction only once.

There is only one correct solution, and you can solve it without guessing. Take your time and enjoy!

Take a look at this example solution to see how it works:

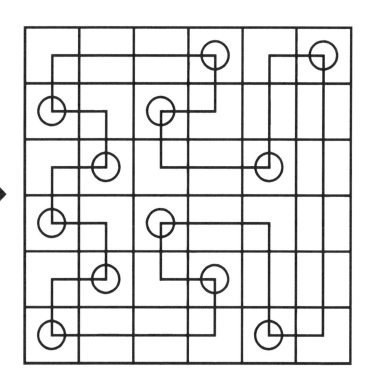

Puzzle #1

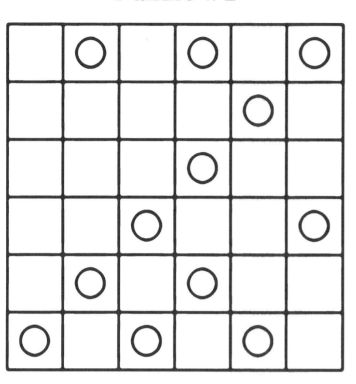

Puzzle #2

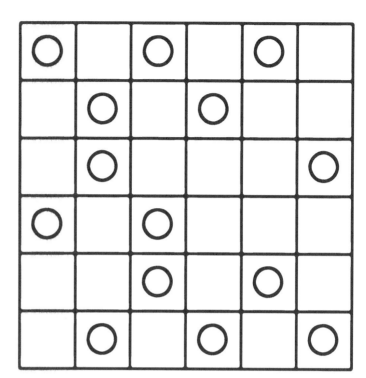

Puzzle #3

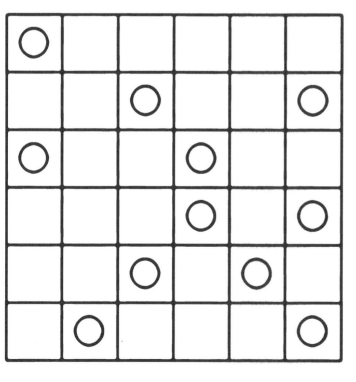

Puzzle #4

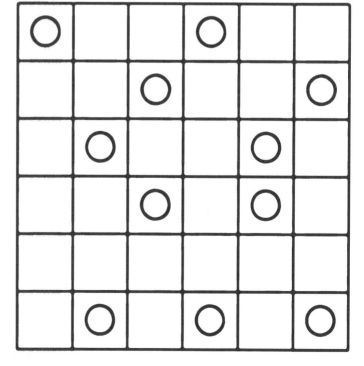

Puzzle #5

Puzzle #6

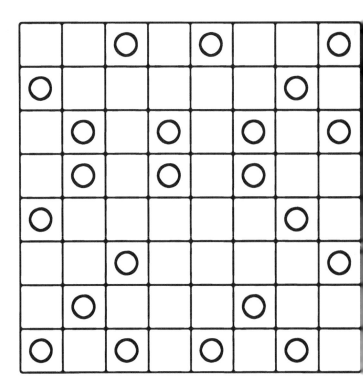

Puzzle #7

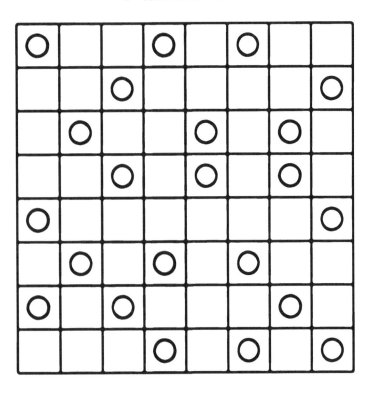

Puzzle #8

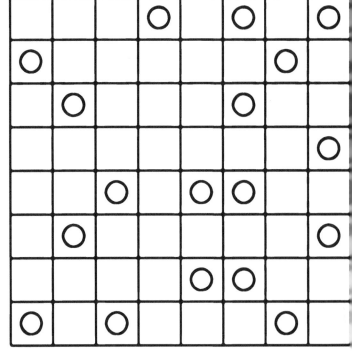

Puzzle #9

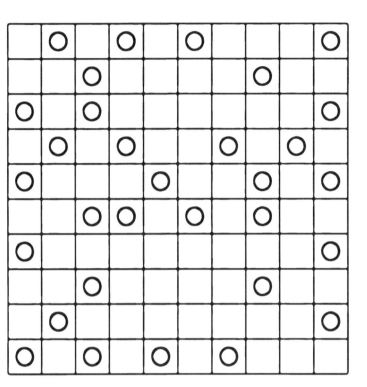

Puzzle #10

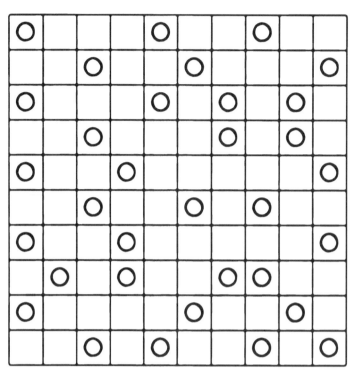

Puzzle #11

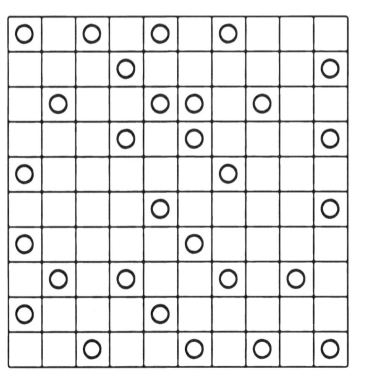

Puzzle #12

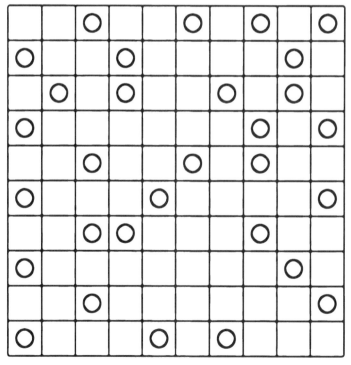

Puzzle #13

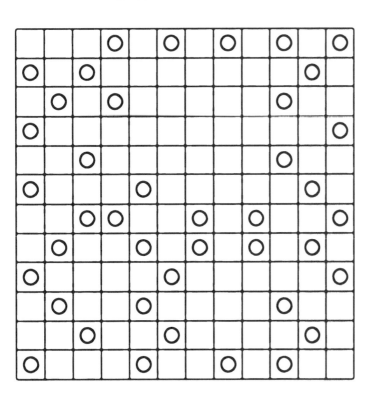

Puzzle #14

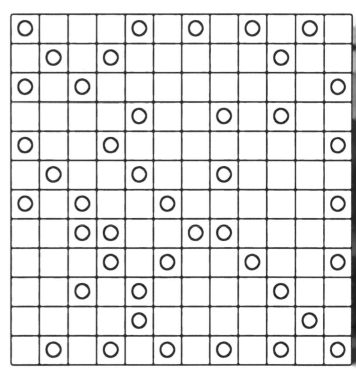

Puzzle #15

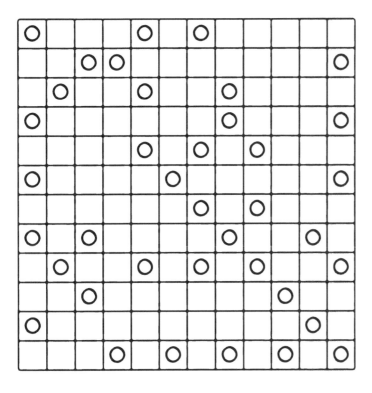

Puzzle #16

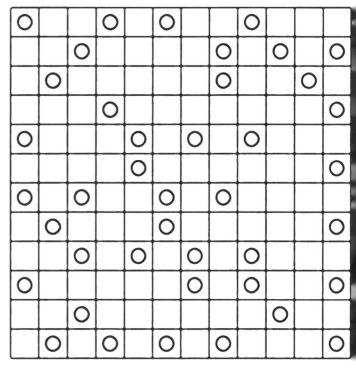

Puzzle #17

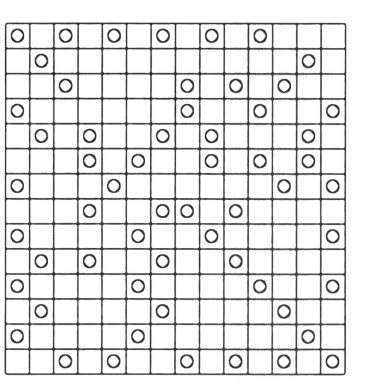

Puzzle #18

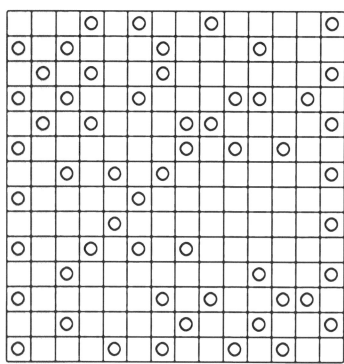

Puzzle #19

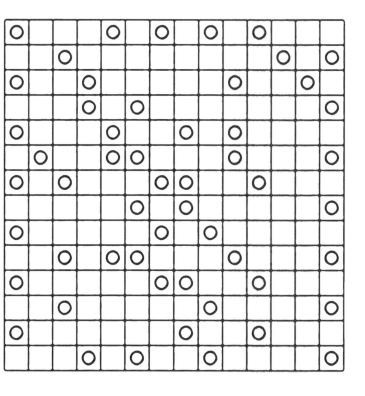

Puzzle #20

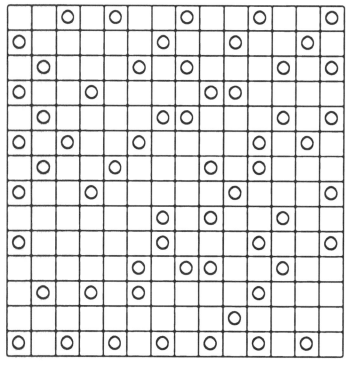

Cryptogram puzzles

A cryptogram is a type of puzzle where every letter in a sentence or phrase has been substituted with a different letter or number. Your task is to figure out which letters have been swapped and decode the hidden message. Don't worry—solving cryptograms can be a lot of fun and a great way to keep your mind sharp!

How to Solve Cryptograms: Simple Steps

Look for Single-Letter Words: In English, the most common single-letter words are "A" and "I." If you see a word made up of just one letter, it's very likely to be one of these.

Common Letters: The six most frequently used letters in English are E, T, A, O, I, N. Look for the letter that appears the most often in the cryptogram, as it's likely one of these.

Look for Common Words: Simple two- or three-letter words are great clues. Words like "TO," "IN," "IS," "THE," "AND," and "FOR" often appear in cryptograms.

Double Letters: Keep an eye out for repeated letters like "LL" in "WILL" or "SS" in "PASS." These are helpful clues that can guide your decoding.

Apostrophes: Words with apostrophes often follow predictable patterns. For example, "IT'S," "CAN'T," or "I'M" are common in English, and recognizing this can help you solve the puzzle.

Stuck? No Worries!

If you find yourself stuck, don't worry! Helpful hints have been provided at the end of this cryptogram puzzles section on page 69 to get you back on track

Puzzle #1

BRWU HQE MDW VQEDOJUF M UJVW

FJDY MU RQED ZWWKZ YJCW M

ZWVQUI. BRWU HQE ZJO QU M DWI

RQO VJUIWD M ZWVQUI ZWWKZ

YJCW MU RQED. ORMO'Z

DWYMOJSJOH.   — Einstein

Puzzle #2

EBGFG AX WUEBAWC AW EBG PUFDI

JUFG XEZNNUFW EBYW Y HUFMXG: TUZ

HYW BAE AE, TUZ HYW LWUHL AE EU

MAGHGX, NZE TUZ HYWWUE HUWQAWHG

AE.   — Alexander Herzen

59

Puzzle #3

OVDFD DBAWOW YR KRUAOAGAXY AY

AYHAX HXFAYM DYRIMV OR XOODZKO

OR DBKUXAY OR OVD ZXWWDW OVXO

GRNW GXY ED DXODY   — **Indira Gandhi**

Puzzle #4

QMYIY WN MCSUYI BDI DIPWSVIJ GIYVP, VSP

QMYIY WN MCSUYI BDI TDKY, BDI ZWSPSYNN,

BDI QMDCUMQBCTSYNN; VSP QMWN WN QMY

UIYVQ ADKYIQJ QMVQ OVZYN AYDATY NCBBYI

ND OCEM.   — **Mother Teresa**

Puzzle #5

NO NL Z VSKKSCEAZVU OMZO OMU MNLOSHT

SD VNYNANRZONSC NL AZHJUAT OMU

MNLOSHT SD QUZESCL.   — **George Orwell**

Puzzle #6

GBF BIS GDPSR PB PGLIX BJ BISRSVJ DR

DVBIS. GBF BIS DEBLQR LP. LP RSSUR

PB LUKVT OSNSWPLBI BO AIKBKAVDOLPT.

— **Anne Morrow Lindbergh**

Puzzle #7

SUTL MNCL, UM XBVLJ UM ZXMMKEOL, GXN

UCL YXKJH MXSLVWKJH GXN'Y EL WUZZG VX

YKL YXKJH.

— **Matt Haig**

Puzzle #8

LTS QEYFG XW NMFF EN HIZXRIF LTXOZW

AILXSOLFU QIXLXOZ NEY EMY QXLW LE ZYEQ

WTIYASY.

— **Bertrand Russell**

Puzzle #9

RPLJSKZS, LOPL AESKTJKN QD BQWPE

ZQFWPNS XJLO ROGCJZPE LJBJTJLG.

— **Thomas Hardy**

Puzzle #10

YE KUSSRB HD SHCR UZ PZHPZ. RLRTE

BHYR H PVRZ HB, HB YUCRD YR FTE.

Puzzle #11

B QKBLACQ KJ HRJD B SRLN AI OABS

DYBD QKQ VMSS RCQMP NPMJJRPM.

Puzzle #12

H VTUA FAHEY XOLLHAC. HS'I IT YLAOS ST

ZHEC SJOS TEA IDAMHOV DALITE GTP QOES

ST OEETG ZTL SJA LAIS TZ GTPL VHZA.

-**Rita Rudner**

Puzzle #13

L'B VKGA L ADE'U WGMJ UD WTEU ODQ

BP DZE ODDA. L WGMJ ED LAJG ZWJQJ

FGEAZLIWJF KLMJ.

Puzzle #14

ZLEAQGQB KYD'BQ TYXFP, EHZEKN PXGQ

100%. DFHQNN KYD'BQ TYFEAXFP JHYYT

Puzzle #15

RWO'M BWXXK. HG TYDO D

RWZLO'M BWXE, MIZXZ DXZ 25

NWXZ YZMMZXL HO MIZ DYTIDVZM.

Puzzle #16

R SHRWG XC LOGM CXKMH

EMCEPM LCHM RWXMHMZXRWV

-Ernest Hemingway

Puzzle #17

IFBM ZWL'OB UM XYUK, Y RWWS

AOUBMS IUKK EB COZUMR CW EYUK ZWL

WLC. Y EBJC AOUBMS IUKK EB UM CFB

TBKK MBHC CW ZWL JYZUMR, 'SYNM,

CFYC IYJ ALM.'   -Groucho Marx

Puzzle #18

PX BTZKHJM CKAA PK Z GFUK FH

ZHCZPFNX RTWVAKP. VEC CGKX JWH'C

TKFAAX QHWD PK.   -Garry Shandling

Puzzle #19

MLC YCOKCM FT YMVRNWP RFBWP NY

MF ENDC LFWCYMER, CVM YEFHER, VWG

ENC VXFBM RFBK VPC.   -Lucille Ball

64

Puzzle #20

INRXKN WXP CYKKW Y HNKAXF, WXP

AJXPET RZKAV CYDN VJNC PAN Y

SXCHPVNK BZVJ AEXB ZFVNKFNV

ANKUZSN VX ANN BJX VJNW KNYEEW

YKN.   **-Will Ferrell**

Puzzle #21

R SEZI AQ IRHX MRW UEFHXZEM. HXTH'M

XFI R NZTEKZV HF VTKLZ: ITRHRKS OFE

HXZ UTHXEFFC.   **-Bob Hope**

Puzzle #22

QUOUG MPY FLL YDII YFJFGGFK KCXY

SFP RXQ ZF YCU ZXS XLYUG YFJFGGFK

APBY XB KUII.   **-Mark Twain**

Puzzle #23

YFUD MEL DUDS QECJPDK CYFC

FQMGEKM KSJUJQI XOEBDS CYFQ MEL

JX FQ JKJEC, FQK FQMEQD IEJQI

RFXCDS CYFQ MEL JX F ZFQJFP?

-George Carlin

Puzzle #24

N FKZT BHFGXGPF GP FET IZQ SEB

MNCCP BMM N PVQPLKNHTK NYO

NMFTK 50 MCBBKP FEGYVP FB

EGXPTCM – STCC, PB MNK PB IBBO!

Puzzle #25

GIMKWKI CKFA DKP AKIHF

GDB JQKSIFZA, SVP PWFD

GXGLD, DFLPWFQ CKFA ZLIU.

Puzzle #26

LH OB VFLB, OBJDILB AZB VHSMW

TBBWL CHSB VFLWHC, DTW FY GHI

JDTTHA OB VFLB, USBABTW AH OB

LHCBHTB VZH FL VFLB, DTW AZBT KILA

OBZDEB MFQB AZBG VHIMW.

-Neil Gaiman

Puzzle #27

OZBWB PY ETAQ ETB OZPTM PT

OZB VEWAX VEWYB OZCT RBPTM

OCALBX CREIO, CTX OZCO PY

TEO RBPTM OCALBX CREIO.

-Oscar Wilde

	Hints	
Puzzle #1	D decodes to R	/	G decodes to O.
Puzzle #2	G decodes to E	/	Y decodes to A.
Puzzle #3	D decodes to E	/	O decodes to T.
Puzzle #4	G decodes to T	/	V decodes to A.
Puzzle #5	O decodes to T	/	U decodes to E.
Puzzle #6	D decodes to A	/	P decodes to T.
Puzzle #7	U decodes to A	
Puzzle #8	S decodes to E	/	L decodes to T
Puzzle #9	S decodes to E	
Puzzle #10	Y decodes to M	/	P decodes to O.
Puzzle #11	Q decodes to D	/	R decodes to U.
Puzzle #12	V decodes to L	/	A decodes to E.
Puzzle #13	B decodes to M	
Puzzle #14	F decodes to N	
Puzzle #15	W decodes to O	
Puzzle #16	M decodes to E	
Puzzle #17	S decodes to D	/	Y decodes to A.
Puzzle #18	P decodes to M	
Puzzle #19	N decodes to I	/	C decodes to E.
Puzzle #20	X decodes to O	/	V decodes to T.
Puzzle #21	T decodes to A	/	F decodes to O.
Puzzle #22	D decodes to I	/	X decodes to A.
Puzzle #23	F decodes to A	/	D decodes to E.
Puzzle #24	B decodes to O	/	T decodes to E.
Puzzle #25	S decodes to B	/	P decodes to T.
Puzzle #26	B decodes to E	/	D decodes to A.
Puzzle #27	E decodes to O	/	C decodes to A.

Sudoku

Easy #1

	1				8			
2				7				
4	8	7			6			
1	3						8	
7		8				9		4
	4						1	2
			6			8	9	3
				9				6
			1				7	

Easy #2

		9			3		4	7
	5			9			1	
			7				9	
2		5			1			
			8					
			3			7		1
	4				6			
	1			3			2	
6	7		9			8		

Easy #3

2				1				
					8		4	
	9		3			7		8
	3	6		4	9			
7								4
			1	2		9	6	
5		4			1		8	
	1		4					
				6				5

Easy #4

					5	9		
5			8	2				4
1		9					2	
6	5				3			
7								9
			7				1	6
	2					6		1
4				5	1			3
		3	9					

Easy #5

			7					
7	1			4		5		
	9				5		6	
3		7	6					5
2								9
6					7	2		3
	7		3				9	
		4		5			8	6
					4			

Easy #6

3				5		6	1	
6		9						
		4	2					
					4	7		
7		8	6		1	2		9
		1	5					
					3	1		
						9		2
	8	2		9				5

Medium #1

9	1						4	
		7		3		1		
					6			7
					1	8	7	3
1								6
3	7	5	9					
4			3					
		1		8		9		
	6						1	8

Medium #2

1						4		9
		6	5		4			1
	4				7		2	
			6					5
		9				1		
7					8			
	7		8				4	
9			7		3	2		
5		1						7

Medium #3

	3	2		7		5	9	
8								
						1		3
7			9				6	
			2	8	4			
	1				7			2
2		4						
								5
	7	3		5		8	1	

Medium #4

	1	7		4				
		6		7				8
		4	5	3				
	3					5		2
	5						3	
9		8					4	
				5	3	9		
8				1		4		
				9		7	2	

Medium #5

		9			7	6		
4			8					
		7					1	4
7						4		9
		2	3		6	1		
5		1						6
1	5					8		
					9			5
		6	5			3		

Medium #6

			1			4	6	
8				6		2		
	6	5						
		7		2	3			
3		8				5		6
			4	8		9		
						1	9	
		6		4				3
	8	1			5			

Hard #1

					5	8		7
	5		4		7			9
				9				
8						5	7	
		5	2		3	9		
	2	9						3
				6				
2			3		4		6	
6		8	7					

Hard #2

	2			4			6	
		9	2			1		
			1				5	2
			5			4		
7				6				3
		6			1			
4	1				8			
		2			5	3		
	6			2			7	

Hard #3

			2	7			1	
	7							3
		3	9	1			4	
		2					9	7
5								2
1	9					8		
	2			8	6	3		
3							2	
	5			4	2			

Hard #4

4	1		7					
		6		4				7
		5			9		2	
3					4			
			8	5	6			
			9					5
	3		6			5		
5				7		9		
					2		8	6

Hard #5

6	5				1	7		
								6
		7		5	9			
1		5				9		
	7			4			5	
		3				1		4
			3	1		2		
2								
		1	8				9	3

Hard #6

7					8	6		
5						9	2	
							7	5
			6		7			
	6	5		9		7	1	
			1		4			
2	3							
	5	9						1
		1	9					6

Hard #7

						5		4
		6	3		5			9
	7				2			
	4			6		2		
	6		5		7		1	
		2		4			7	
			2				5	
8			6		9	1		
5		7						

Hard #8

2						8	5	
	9				1			7
			6		4			3
			8	9		4		
	8						7	
		2		6	5			
9			4		8			
6			7				2	
	4	5						8

Trivia Quizzes

Test your knowledge with these fun and challenging trivia questions! Each question comes with three possible answers. Choose the answer you think is correct, and check your knowledge as you go along. There's no rush, so take your time and enjoy the quiz!

1. What three crops, when planted together, are known as the "Three Sisters?"

A) Corn, beans, and squash
B) Wheat, barley, and rye
C) Rice, oats, and millet

2. How many bones are in the human body?

A) 206
B) 210
C) 300

3. What are the ingredients in a Boulevardier?

A) Gin, vermouth, and Campari
B) Bourbon, Campari, and sweet vermouth
C) Vodka, triple sec, and lime juice

4. Who painted the Sistine Chapel?

A) Leonardo da Vinci
B) Michelangelo
C) Raphael

5.How many hearts does an octopus have?

A) 2
B) 3
C) 4

6.Who is known as the "Father of Medicine"?

A) Hippocrates
B) Socrates
C) Plato

7.Which planet is known as the "Morning Star"?

A) Venus
B) Mars
C) Saturn

8.How many rings are on the Olympic flag?

A) 4
B) 5
C) 6

9.What year was the first iPhone released?

A) 2005
B) 2007
C) 2010

10. What year did the Berlin Wall fall?

A) 1985
B) 1989
C) 1991

11. What is the chemical symbol for gold?

A. Au
B. Ag
C. Fe

12. Which state has the northernmost latitude in the contiguous states?

A) Alaska
B) Minnesota
C) Washington

13. In Major League Baseball, how far is it from the pitcher's mound to home plate?

A) 45 feet
B) 60 feet, 6 inches
C) 75 feet

14. Who declined the 1964 Nobel Prize for Literature?

A) Jean-Paul Sartre
B) Albert Camus
C) Gabriel García Márquez

15. What is the British dish of sausages and mashed potatoes better known as in the UK?

A) Bubble and squeak
B) Bangers and mash
C) Shepherd's pie

16. What did Jack Dempsey do before he was a boxer?

A) He was a copper miner.
B) He was a school teacher.
C) He was a lawyer.

17. What is the name of the oldest commissioned warship still afloat?

A) HMS Victory
B) USS Arizona
C) The USS Constitution

18. What branch of the US Military boasts the Blue Angels?

A) Navy
B) Air Force
C) Marines

19. What is the most abundant element in the universe?

A) Oxygen
B) Carbon
C) Hydrogen

20. Who said, "Well done is better than well said?"

A) Abraham Lincoln
B) Benjamin Franklin
C) Mark Twain

21. What is the geographically largest US state?

A) Texas
B) Alaska
C) California

22. What movie famously ends with the line, "Well, nobody's perfect?"

A) Some Like It Hot
B) Casablanca
C) Gone with the Wind

23. What are the three flavors in Neapolitan ice cream?

A) Chocolate, vanilla, and strawberry
B) Chocolate, strawberry, and mint
C) Vanilla, chocolate, and caramel

24. What was the name of the very first Saturday morning cartoon?

A) Mighty Mouse
B) Crusader Rabbit
C) Tom and Jerry

25. What breakfast cereal commercial's dialog ended with the line, "He likes it. Hey Mikey!"

A) Life cereal
B) Cheerios
C) Frosted Flakes

26. What was Charlotte's first message in her web in Charlotte's Web?

A) Some Pig
B) Terrific
C) Radiant

27. What soft drink was billed as "the real thing?"

A) Pepsi
B) Coca Cola
C) Dr. Pepper

28. Which ingredient do you adjust in a martini to make it dry or wet?

A) Vodka
B) Olive juice
C) Vermouth

29. Which fast food restaurant's commercial asked, "Where's the beef?"

A) Burger King
B) McDonald's
C) Wendy's

30. What type of dog is Scooby Doo?

A) Great Dane
B) Boxer
C) Mastiff

31. What type of fruit is a pomelo?

A) Berry
B) Citrus
C) Stone fruit

32. What type of moss hangs from tree branches throughout the South?

A) Reindeer moss
B) Spanish moss
C) Club moss

33. Where is the tallest known living tree in the world located?

A) Sequoia National Park
B) Redwood National Park
C) Yosemite National Park

34. What are the three states of matter?

A) Solid, liquid, gas
B) Liquid, vapor, ice
C) Matter, energy, plasma

35. What is the first thing you solve in math's order of operations?

A) Exponents
B) Multiplication
C) Parentheses

36. What is the most populated U.S. state?

A) New York
B) California
C) Texas

37. What country makes the most wine?

A) Italy
B) France
C) United States

38. In basketball, when you dribble the ball with both hands, what is it called?

A) Carrying
B) Double dribble
C) Traveling

39. What airline did Northwest Airlines merge with in 2010?

A) Delta
B) American Airlines
C) United Airlines

40. What is the process by which plants make their own food using sunlight?

A) Respiration
B) Photosynthesis
C) Fermentation

41. Which mountain range is the longest in the world?

A) Himalayas
B) Andes
C) Rockies

42. What is the process by which rocks, soil, and sediments are moved by wind, water, or ice?

A) Weathering
B) Deposition
C) Erosion

43. Which gas makes up the majority of Earth's atmosphere?

A) Oxygen
B) Nitrogen
C) Carbon dioxide

44. What is the national animal of Scotland?

A) Lion
B) Unicorn
C) Eagle

45. What is the largest living species of lizard?

A) Gila Monster
B) Komodo Dragon
C) Iguana

46. Who was the second President of the United States?

A) Thomas Jefferson
B) John Adams
C) George Washington

47. Who was the UK's longest serving female Prime Minister?

A) Theresa May
B) Margaret Thatcher
C) Elizabeth II

48. What type of pastry is made to create profiteroles?

A) Filo
B) Puff
C) Choux

49. What does the car company BMW stand for in English?

A) British Motor Works
B) Bavarian Motor Works
C) Berlin Motor Works

50. Which aniseed flavored drink is the national drink of Greece?

A) Ouzo
B) Sambuca
C) Absinthe

Labyrinths

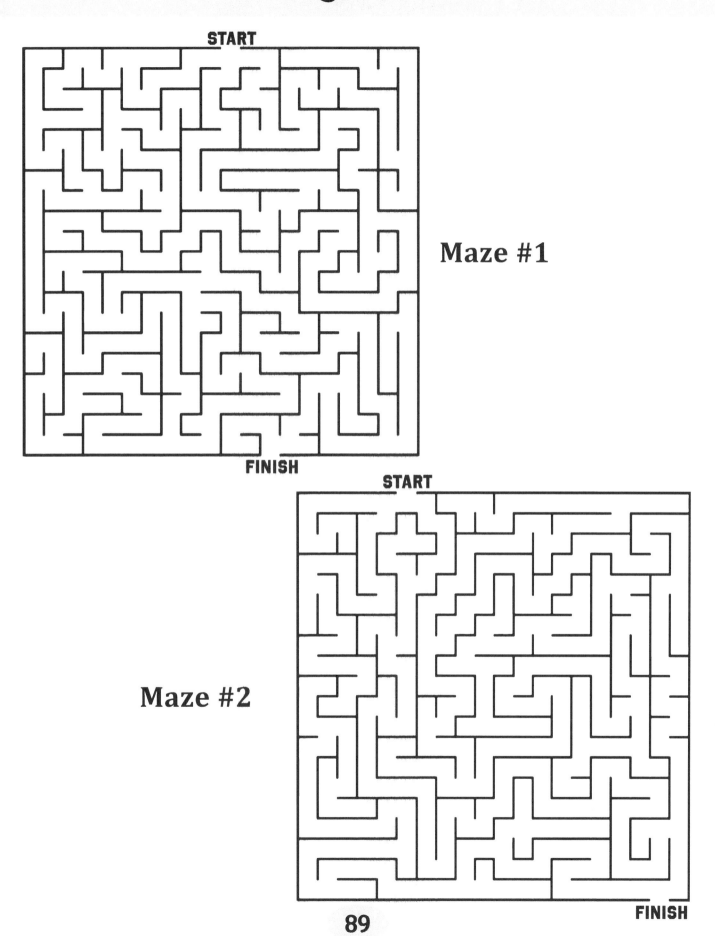

START

Maze #1

FINISH

START

Maze #2

FINISH

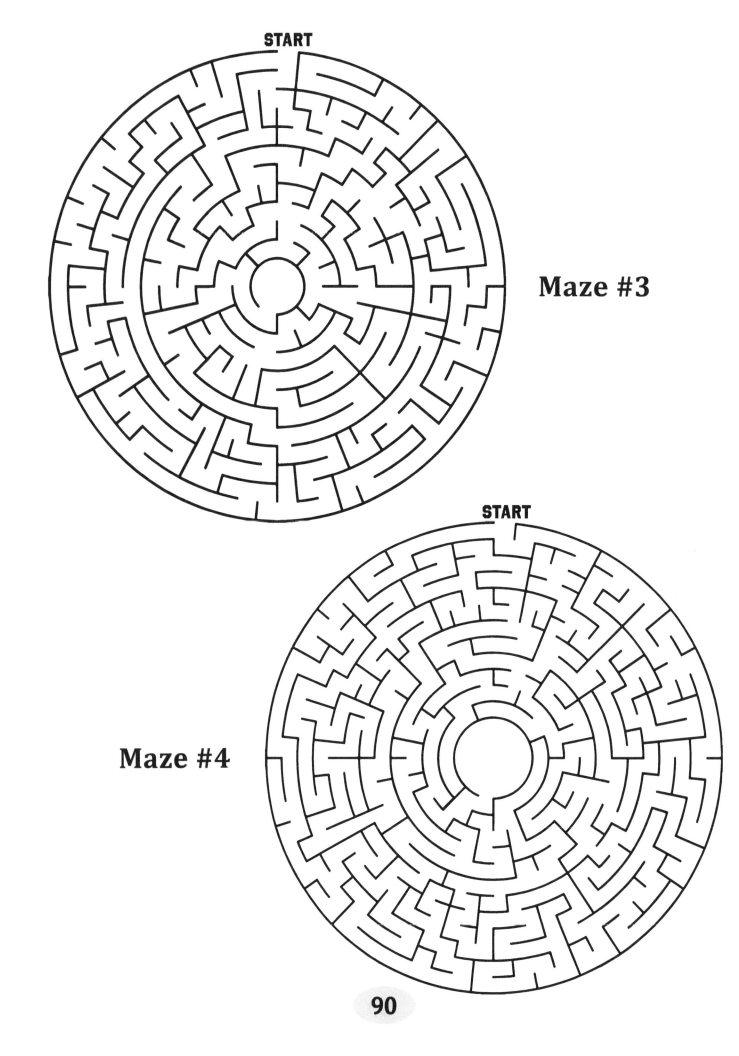

START

Maze #3

START

Maze #4

Maze #5

Maze #6

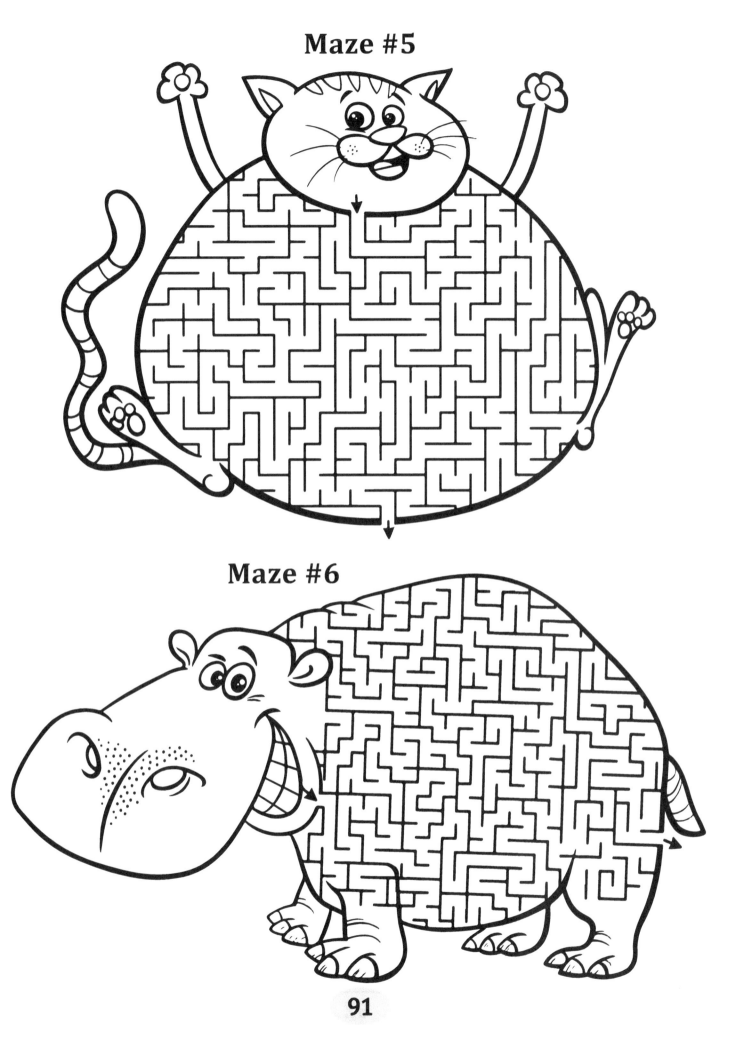

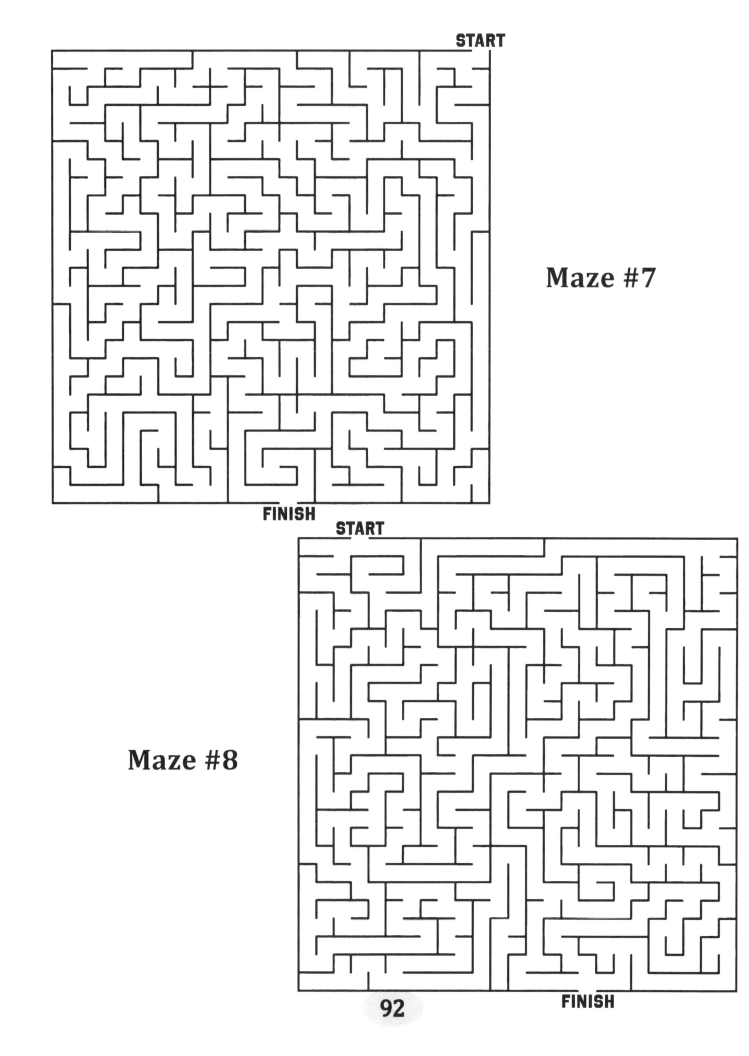

START

Maze #7

FINISH

START

Maze #8

FINISH

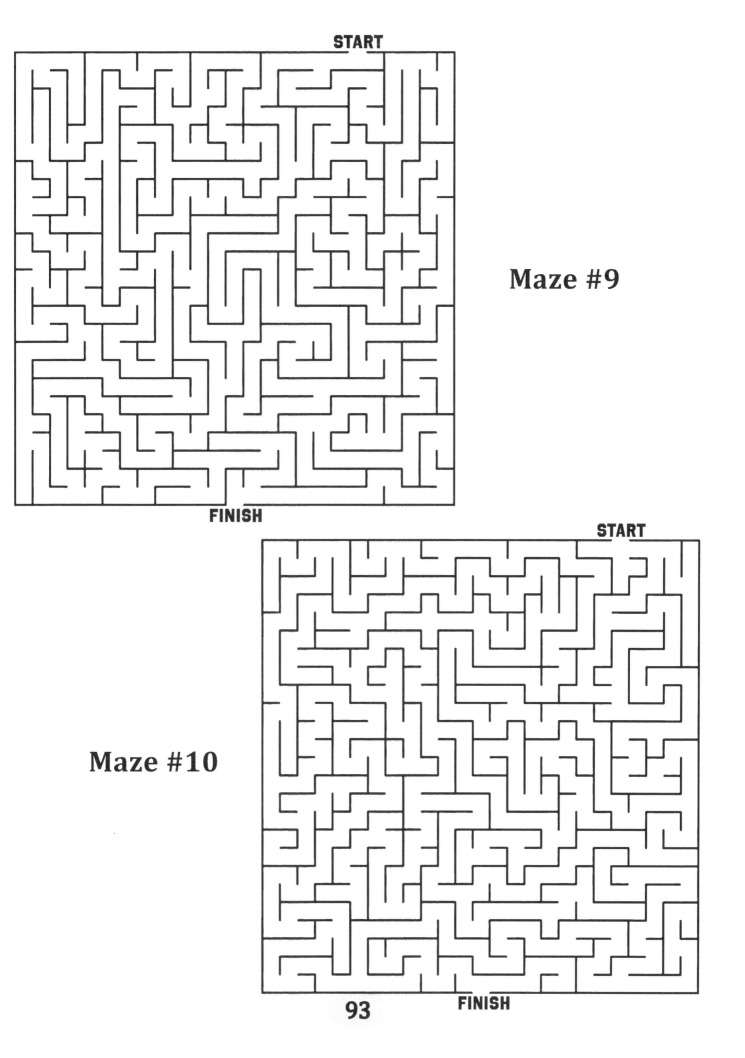

START

Maze #9

FINISH

START

Maze #10

FINISH

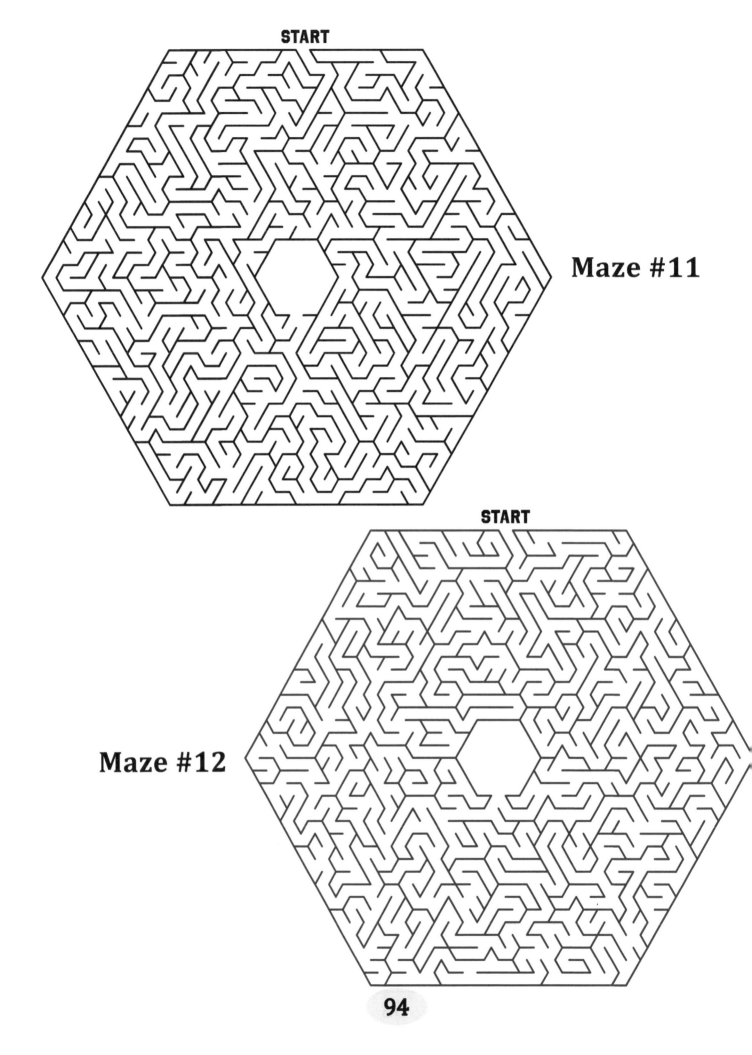

START

Maze #11

START

Maze #12

Maze #13

START

FINISH

Maze #15

START

FINISH

Maze #16

Word Fill-In Puzzles

What is a Word Fill-In Puzzle?

A Word Fill-In Puzzle is similar to a crossword puzzle, but instead of being given clues, you're provided with a list of words. Your task is to place each word into the grid. The challenge is to fit all the words into the puzzle correctly.

How it works:

- Each word is sorted by the number of letters and arranged alphabetically.

- The goal is to fit all the provided words into the grid, ensuring that every word fits without leaving any unused spaces.

Unlike crosswords, where clues are given, in Word Fill-In puzzles, you must figure out where to place the words just by their length and how they intersect with each other.

Puzzle #1

2 Letters

AM
AN
AS
AT
BE
DO
HE
IS
ME
MY
NO
OR
OX
PI
TO
US

3 Letters

ASP
DOC
EGO
EPI
ERE
IDO
JET
OBI
ODA
POD
TEN
YEN

4 Letters

IOWA
IWIS
JIBE
KNIT
NARC
ODIN
STAB
TIDY

5 Letters

BOATS
KYACK
SIXTY
SPECS

7 Letters

BYGONES
KADDISH
METEORS
OEDIPUS

Puzzle #2

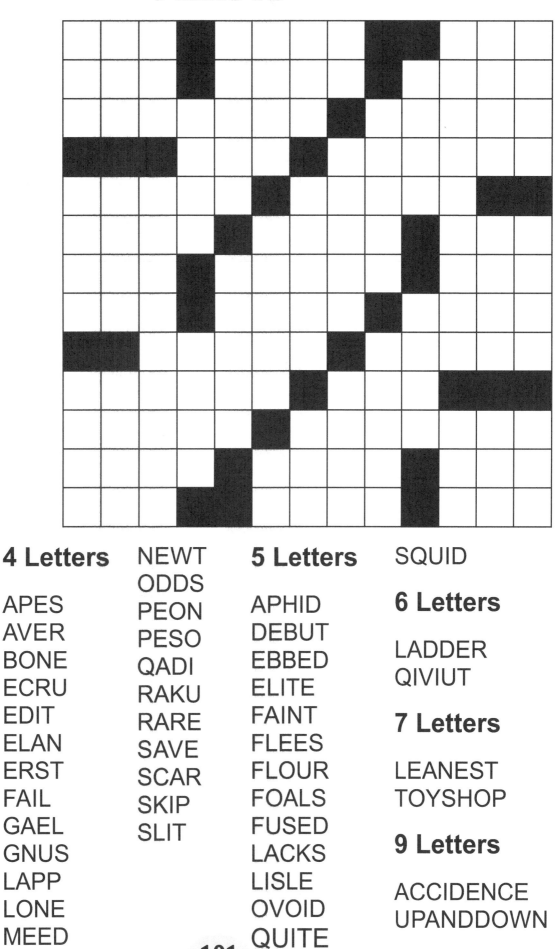

2 Letters

GO
SO

3 Letters

AGE
AGO
APE
ARE
EAR
ERG
ERN
ESP
IDA
KEY
KIN
LAD
MOA
NAN
OAK
OAT
RAT
SPA
TET
TIN

4 Letters

APES
AVER
BONE
ECRU
EDIT
ELAN
ERST
FAIL
GAEL
GNUS
LAPP
LONE
MEED
NEWT
ODDS
PEON
PESO
QADI
RAKU
RARE
SAVE
SCAR
SKIP
SLIT

5 Letters

APHID
DEBUT
EBBED
ELITE
FAINT
FLEES
FLOUR
FOALS
FUSED
LACKS
LISLE
OVOID
QUITE
SQUID

6 Letters

LADDER
QIVIUT

7 Letters

LEANEST
TOYSHOP

9 Letters

ACCIDENCE
UPANDDOWN

Puzzle #3

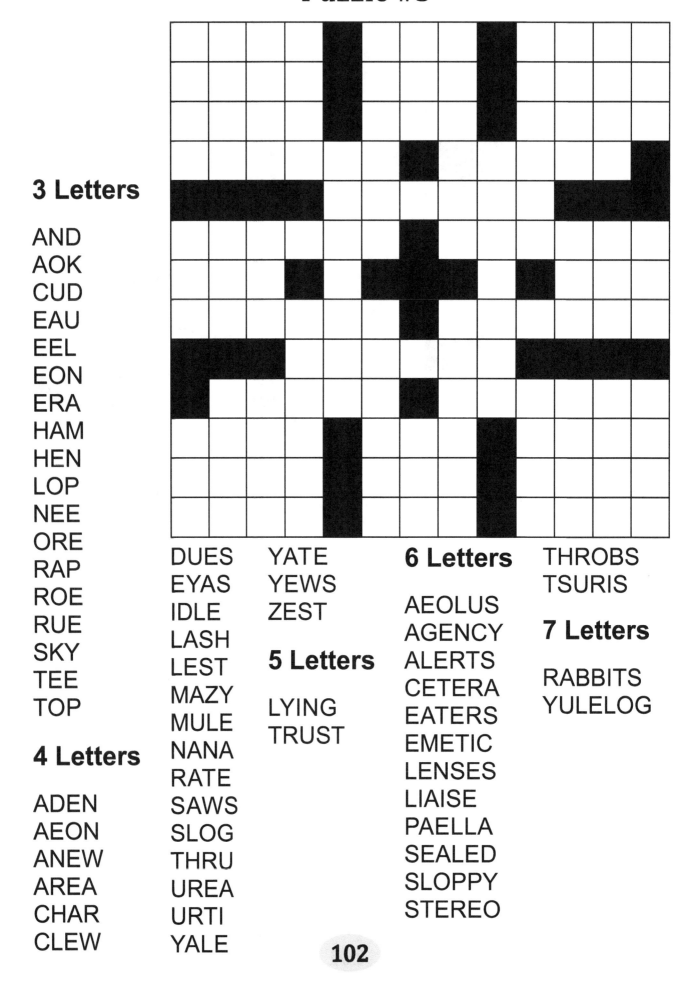

3 Letters

AND
AOK
CUD
EAU
EEL
EON
ERA
HAM
HEN
LOP
NEE
ORE
RAP
ROE
RUE
SKY
TEE
TOP

4 Letters

ADEN
AEON
ANEW
AREA
CHAR
CLEW
DUES
EYAS
IDLE
LASH
LEST
MAZY
MULE
NANA
RATE
SAWS
SLOG
THRU
UREA
URTI
YALE
YATE
YEWS
ZEST

5 Letters

LYING
TRUST

6 Letters

AEOLUS
AGENCY
ALERTS
CETERA
EATERS
EMETIC
LENSES
LIAISE
PAELLA
SEALED
SLOPPY
STEREO
THROBS
TSURIS

7 Letters

RABBITS
YULELOG

Puzzle #4

2 Letters

HI
OK

3 Letters

ADO
BED
DUO
HIE
OAR
ODD
ONO
ORT

SAT
TON

4 Letters

AGED
AINT
BUGS
BUNK
CREE
ERIS
FLOE
HENS
IRIS
OMEN

OUTS
PROD
RENT
SOAK

5 Letters

ESKER
IDLED
PORTS
SEEDY
SLEDS
SODAS
STARK

6 Letters

ASIANS
CARINA
DASHES
DEVOUT
DIETER
ENCYST
ERRATA
FOREST
IDEATE
IRONED
KARATE
LATVIA

MODULE
NEARED
NICEST
NOTARY
ORDEAL
OUSTED
REUBEN
SEAEAR
TALENT
YEASTS

7 Letters

EROSION
GOSLING
TREATED

Puzzle #5

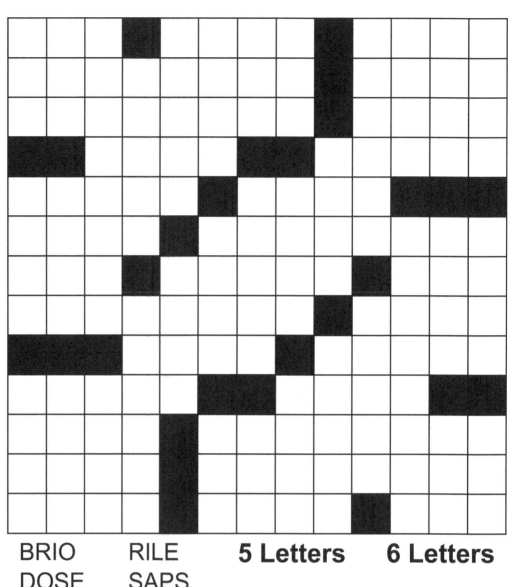

3 Letters

ARE
EYE
FEW
HUG
HUT
MET
ODE
ONE
PRE
SIT
UEY
UNI

4 Letters

ALSO
AMMO
APES
ARID
BETA
BRIO
DOSE
EIRE
GALA
HARP
MITE
OILS
OLIO
OMAR
OMIT
OPAL
PIER
PLAT
RATE
RILE
SAPS
SARI
SCAD
SKIN
SOIL
SORE
SUDD
TENS
USER

5 Letters

WEDS
APERY
BAIZA
BALAS
BIRDS
DOPEY
ONSET
SIREN
SLIER
SOILS
SOUND

6 Letters

HOBNOB
IGNORE

8 Letters

ENDANGER
ETHICIZE
FOULEDUP
GILLETTE
OAKRIDGE
SAILBOAT
TELEPATH
UNESPIED

Puzzle #6

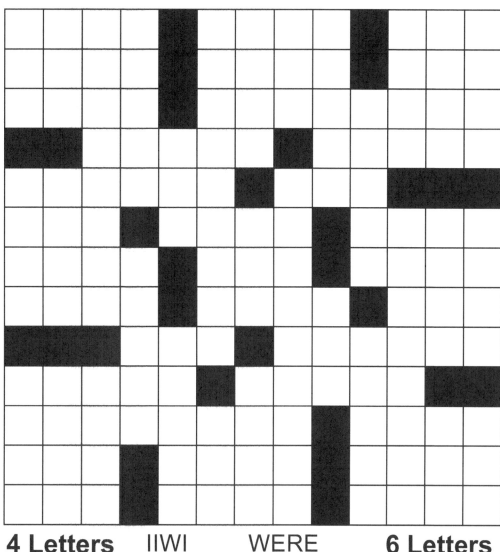

3 Letters

COO
DER
EAR
ERG
ITS
OAT
ORB
ORE
PAS
RIO
ROT
SAC
TAT
TED
TOE
USE
WEN
WIG

4 Letters

ACED
ATOM
COGS
DIET
DUTY
DYES
EDAM
EGGS
EMIT
ETTE
GIST
ICED
IDEA
IIWI
IRKS
KEGS
KNIT
LOAD
OATH
OBIE
ORAL
RAIL
REED
SEWN
SHOT
STYE
TRIO

WERE

5 Letters

WERE
AISLE
ALIKE
ANTRE
DHOLE
EARLY
NANAS
OLEUM
SEPIA
SWAIN
YIELD

6 Letters

IDLERS
REALMS

8 Letters

ETIOLOGY
HECATOMB
NANNYGAI
OUTLYING
SINUSITIS

9 Letters

UTTERABLE

Puzzle #7

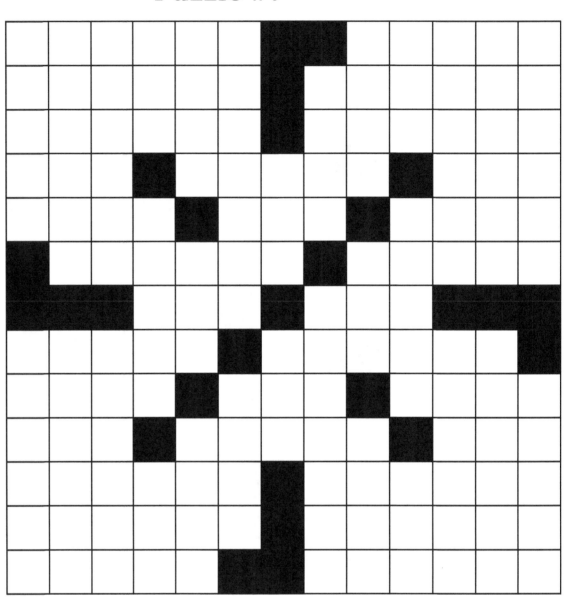

3 Letters

AGO
ALE
ATE
EMU
FEN
FIT
ITS
LEU
LIE
LOT
OAF
SAD
SAO
TAI
TUT
TWA

4 Letters

ATOM
GENE
GRAB
HIES
ILIE
NAIF
PAWN
SAYS
SNOB
SNOW

5 Letters

ARETE
BRIES
DONEE
EOSIN
FOSSE
GAINS
GOUDA
MATES
PARED
PESTS

6 Letters

ATTIRE
AWOKEN
DANUBE
DHARMA
EERILY
ENEMAS
ENLIST
ERRAND
LOWSET
MELONS
NAGANA
NEEDLE
OILIER
ORATOR
PROFIT
RAKERS
RETUNE
RIDLEY
SOIREE
STATIC

SWEETS
TINDAL

7 Letters

LIONESS
TYCOONS

Puzzle #8

3 Letters

AFT
EMU
FEE
HOE
ICE
LEN
LET
MUD
OUD
SEE

4 Letters

ACID
ALMS
AONE
ARIA
AXLE
BLAE
CLIP
DADS
DEED
DENT
DEPT
DHAL
DOUR
EAVE
EDGY
EMIT
EVES
EXAM
FUME
FUTZ
GAPE
GEST

IRON
KEAS
LEAN
MESA
OGEE
OXEN
RIOT
RIPE
SHED
SLIP
SOLD
TELE
THUS

TREE
URIC
WEIR

5 Letters

AGAIN
DRILY
EOSIN
GAPES
HELLO
HIREE
IDEAL

OGIVE
RAMAL
REACT
REBEC
RECUR
SABER
SENTE
SINUS
SLABS
STOPS
TYRES

6 Letters

DOGMAN
EXEMPT
OODLES
REWEDS
RINSED
SHRIEK
STATUE
TWEEZE

7 Letters

SWEEPER
YEREVAN

8 Letters

RUCKSACK
TECTONIC

10 Letters

AEROSPHERE
APOTROPAIC

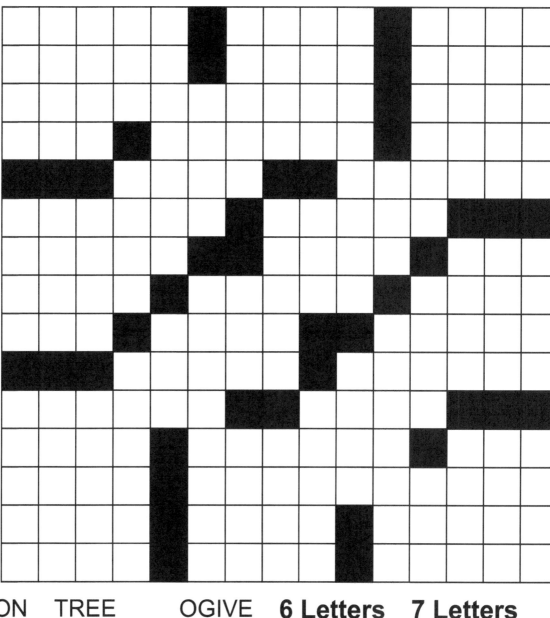

107

Puzzle #9

3 Letters

AWE
ILE
IVE
LAC
LEE
LOO
TEA
UTE

4 Letters

ALEE
APED
ARAB
AREA
AVER
BLOC
CODA
DELL
EASE
EBBS
ELLS
GALE
IDES
ITEM
KELP
KNEW
KOLO
MAMA
MANS
NEMO
NETS
OBIT
OCTO
PINT
PREP
RALE
SEAT
SERE
SLED
SOCK
SPEW
STAG
TAMO
TOAD
UMBO

UTAH

5 Letters

ABIDE
ALONE
AMBER
DERMS
ECLAT
EDGED
EMBER
HOSES
ICIER
LEASE
LICKS
MATTE
NEPAL
PETAL
PLEAS
REOPT
SMOLT
SUOMI
TAILS
TRACK

6 Letters

ABSORB
COOEED
MEDALS
MIRAGE

7 Letters

ERASERS
IRELAND
LANOLIN
STOPPLE

8 Letters

PARSNIPS
TWITCHED

10 Letters

REMAINEDER
TABLECLOTH

11 Letters

PREDISPOSES
TOTALISATOR

Puzzle #10

3 Letters

AIM
ATE
GOA
HEX
LAM
LSD
OPE
SBS
WAR

4 Letters

ABUT
AVID
BLUE
BORA
EDDY
EDNA
EPEE
EPIC
ERNE
ESAU
HERB
HERR
HULK
KENO
LAUD
LUAU
LWEI
MELD
MINK
NECK
OBOE
ODES

OVER
PILL
REAL
ROBE
RUBS
SETS
SUEZ
TOED
TOYS
TREY
TYRE
USSR

WARN
XIAN

5 Letters

ABBEY
AEONS
BLAND
DELTA
DRATS
ENROL
ENSUE
LABOR

LISPS
METHO
NANCE
NORSE
OCEAN
OLDER
PAEON
RANEE
RENEW
SENGI
SEWED
SHAKY

SNEAK
UMBRA
URATE
VALOR
YESIL

6 Letters

DWELLS
ETOILE
IODATE
MULLAH

RELENT
ZENITH

7 Letters

AMERICA
ESTATES

8 Letters

BARTLETT
CLEVERLY

109

Solutions

Memory Games

VIEW FROM ABOVE

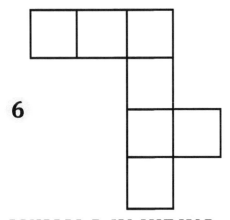

6

FIND TWO IDENTICAL SHAPES

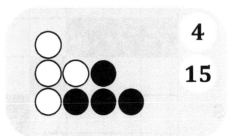

4

15

ANIMALS IN HIDING

1. Rat
2. Camel
3. Cat
4. Cow
5. Deer
6. Dog
7. Fish
8. Frog
9. Goat
10. Horse
11. Lion
12. Monkey
13. Ox
14. Snake
15. Tiger
16. Armadillo

WHAT'S THE WORD?

Easy

Hamster
Banana
Science
Ocean
Slow

Insanely Tough

Hydrogen
Mona Lisa
Sapphire
Triceratops
Eiffel Tower

Getting Tricky

California
Dumbledore
Oak
Violin
Snowboarding

FIND IT

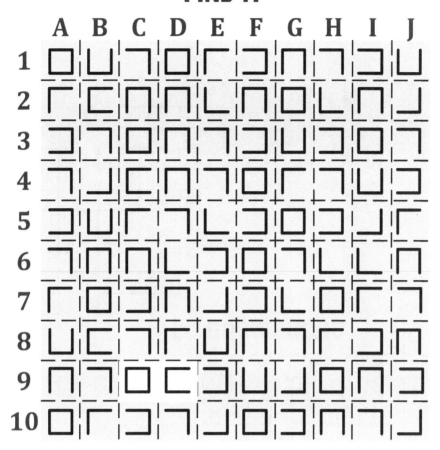

Crossword Puzzles

CROSSWORD #1

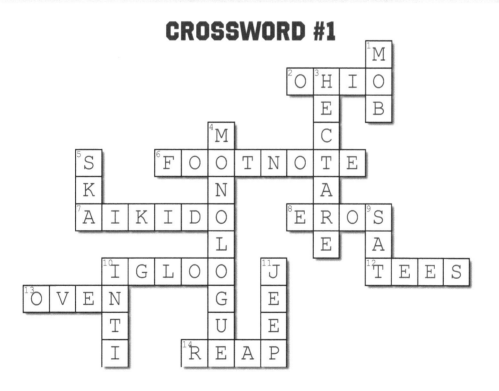

CROSSWORD #2

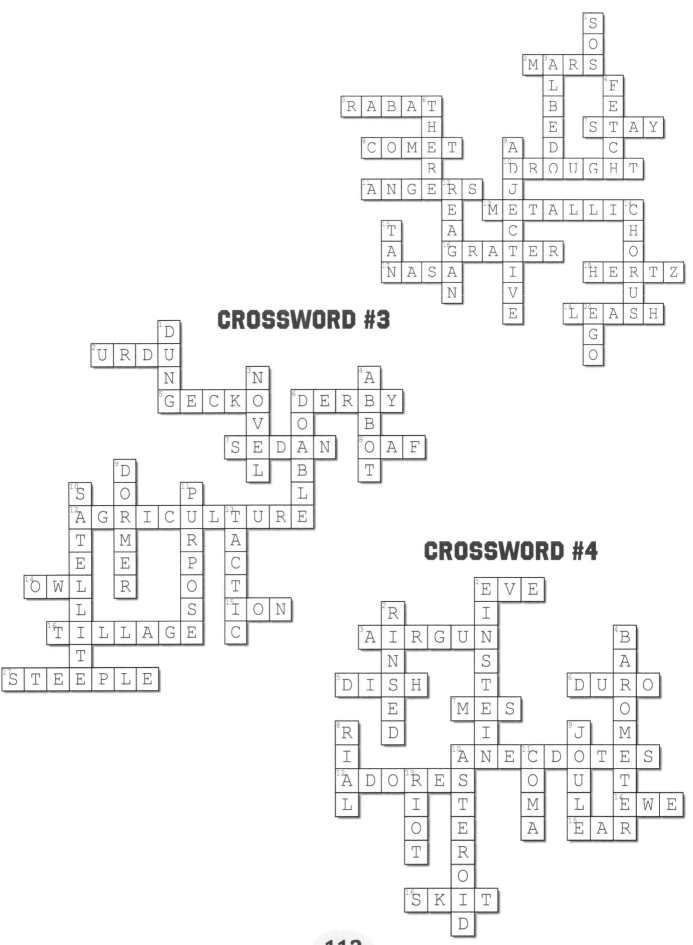

CROSSWORD #3

CROSSWORD #4

CROSSWORD #5

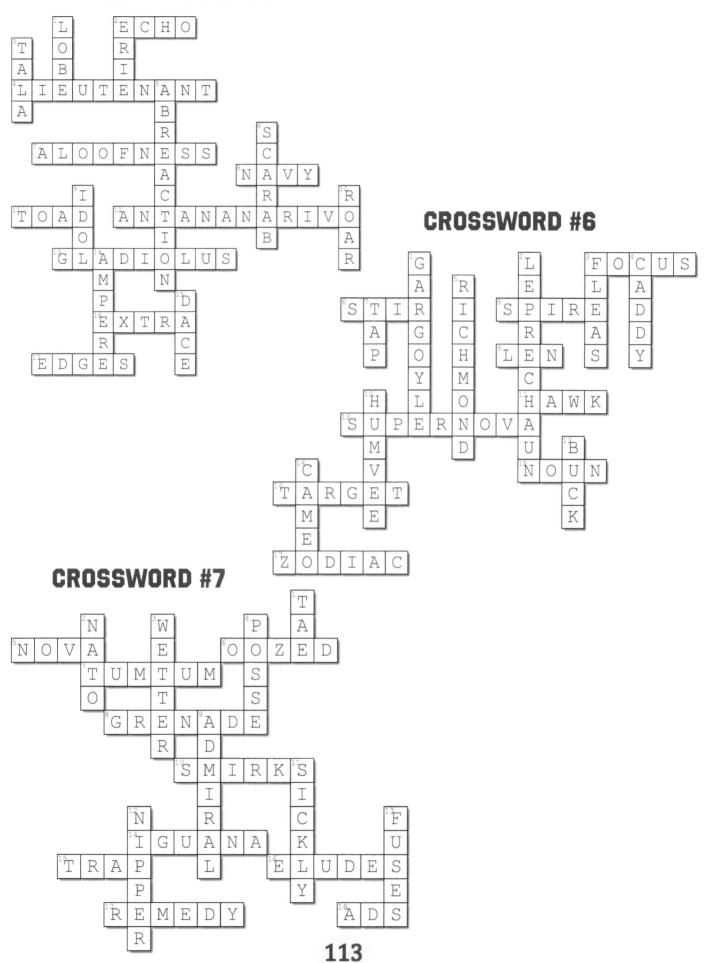

CROSSWORD #6

CROSSWORD #7

113

CROSSWORD #8

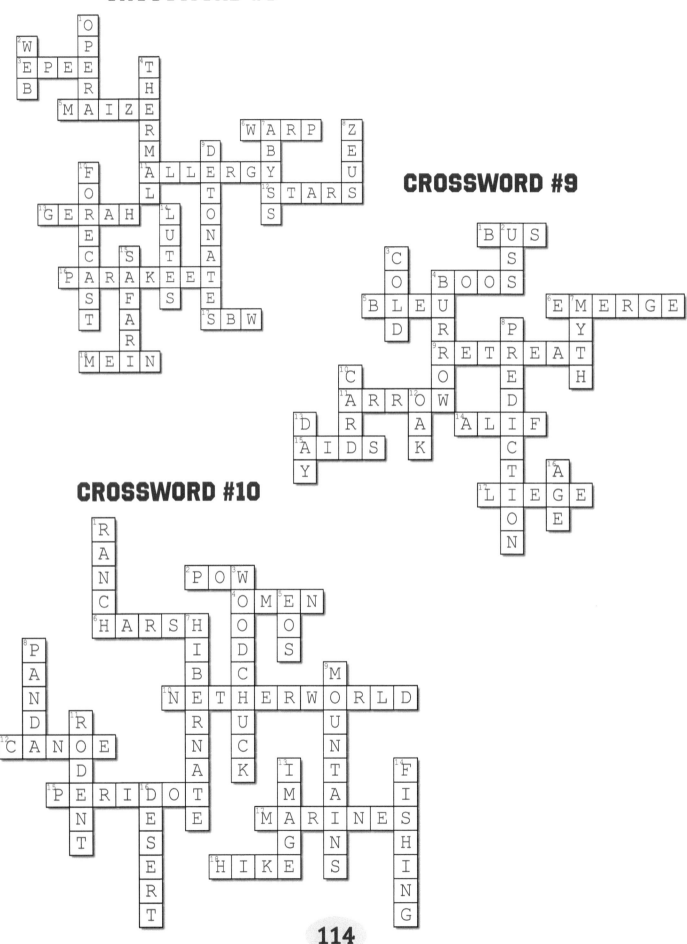

CROSSWORD #9

CROSSWORD #10

114

Logic Puzzles

DOUBLE AND TRIPLE!

1	9	2
3	8	4
7	6	8

CHANGE TWELVE LETTERS

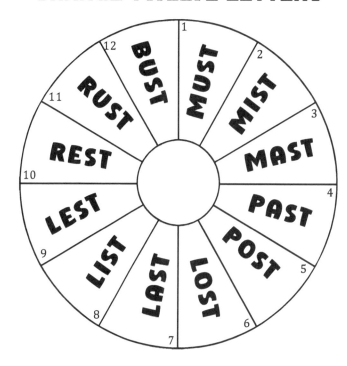

THE RACE AND FAVORITE TV SHOWS

Times	First Names	Tv Shows	Houses
2 min, 59 sec	Emma	Planet Earth	Farmhouse
3 min, 2 sec	Chloe	The Comedy Club	Modern House
3 min, 5 sec	Sam	Mystery Hour	Cottage
3 min, 8 sec	Ben	Wild Adventures	Villa

THE SAFE

- The first clue tells us that the numbers 1, 2, and 3 are not in the combination.

- By looking at the third clue, we can figure out that 6 is in the code.

- The second clue then tells us that 6 is the third number in the combination, and that numbers 4 and 5 are also not in the combination.

- The last clue tells us that either 8 or 9 is in the right spot. But since 9 can't be in that spot because 6 is already there, 8 must be the first number in the combination.

- The second-to-last clue helps us find out that 7 is the second number in the combination.

So the combination is:

8	7	6

UNINTERRUPTED PATH

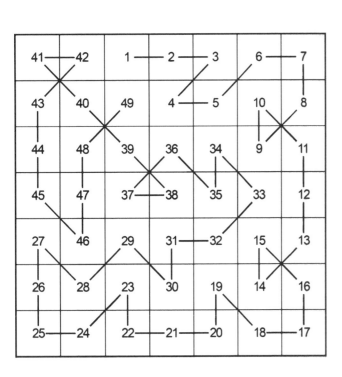

MATCHSTICK PUZZLES

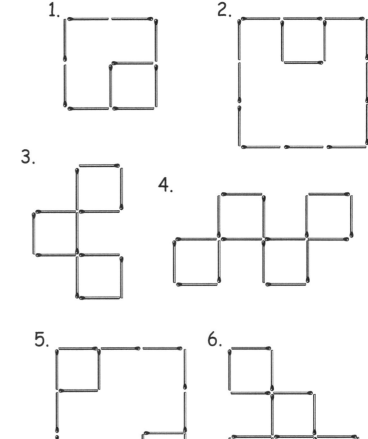

1.

2.

3.

4.

5.

6.

THE LASER BEAM PUZZLE

3 Possible Solutions

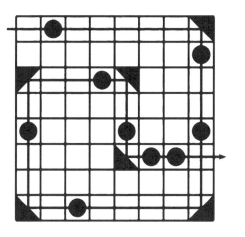 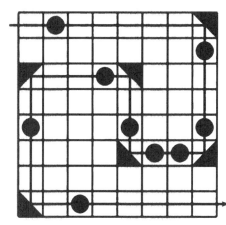 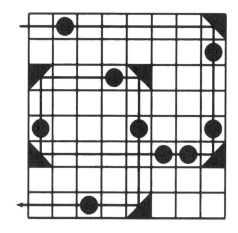

TEA TIME LOGIC PUZZLE

Last Day Of Work	First Names	Hobbies	Teas
January 31	Avery	painting	black tea
February 19	Elijah	reading	white tea
June 12	Angelo	astronomy	green tea
October 23	Jayden	skydiving	herbal tea
December 9	Damian	bicycling	oolong tea

THE TRIANGULAR GARDEN

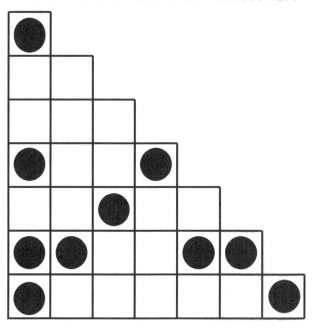

THE GUARDIANS

117

WHO SITS WHERE?

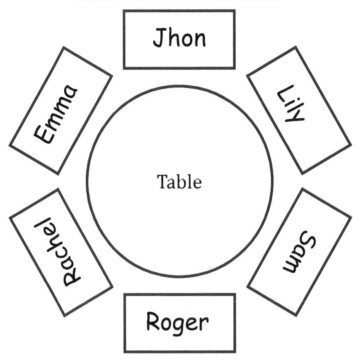

Word Searches

GARDENING

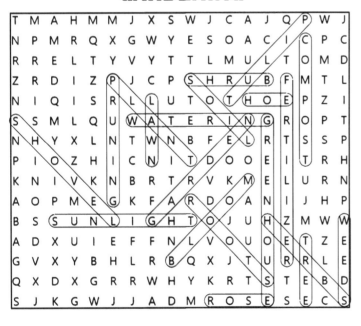

TRAVEL DESTINATIONS

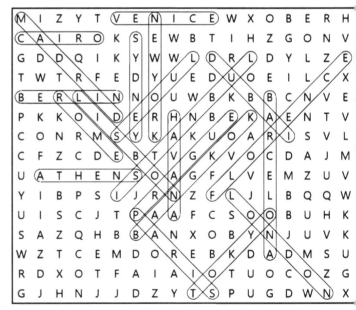

FAMOUS ARTISTS

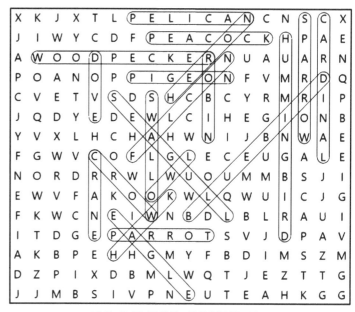

BIRD WATCHING

COOKING INGREDIENTS

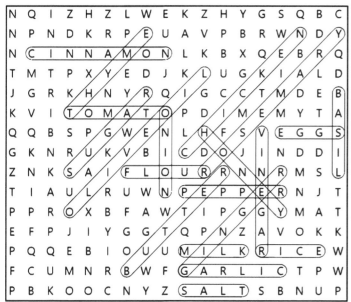

CLASSIC MOVIES

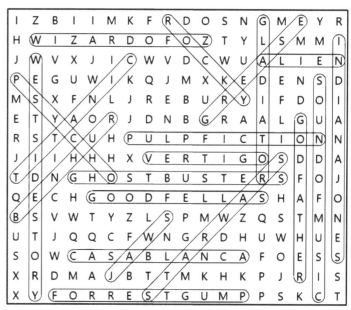

FAMOUS AUTHORS

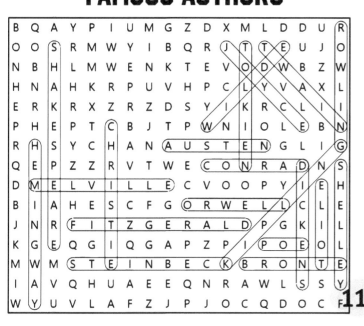

OUTDOOR ACTIVITIES

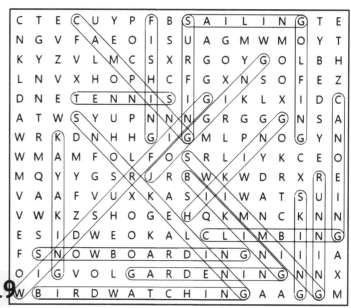

FAMOUS LANDMARKS

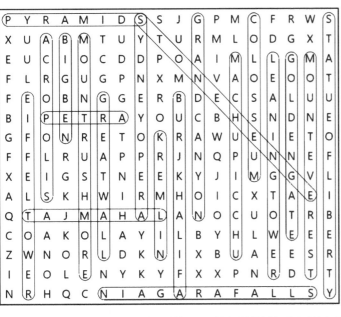

MUSIC INSTRUMENTS

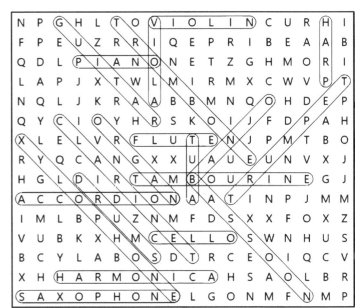

Roundabouts

Puzzle #1

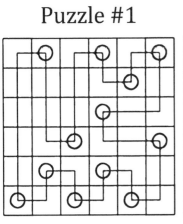

Puzzle #2

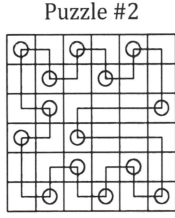

Puzzle #3

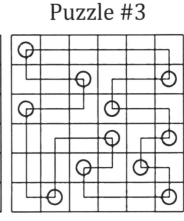

Puzzle #4

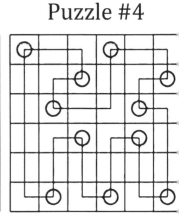

Puzzle #5

Puzzle #6

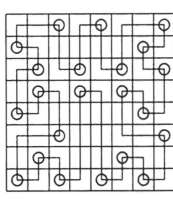

Puzzle #7

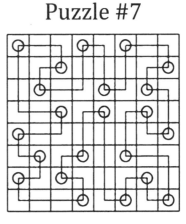

Puzzle #8

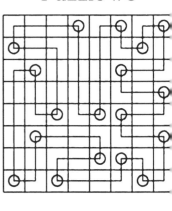

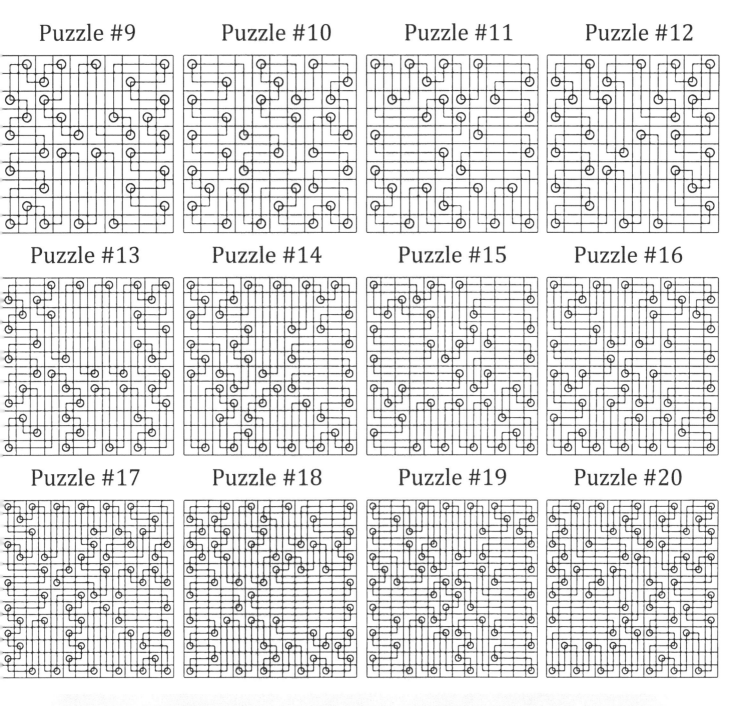

Cryptogram puzzles

Puzzle #1

When You Are Courting A Nice Girl An Hour Seems Like A Second.
When You Sit On A Red Hot Cinder A Second Seems Like An Hour.
That's Relativity.

Puzzle #2

There is nothing in the world more stubborn than a corpse: you can hit it, you can knock it to pieces, but you cannot convince it.

Puzzle #3

There exists no politician in India daring enough to attempt to explain to the masses that cows can be eaten.

Puzzle #4

There is hunger for ordinary bread, and there is hunger for love, for kindness, for thoughtfulness; and this is the great poverty that makes people suffer so much.

Puzzle #5

It is a commonplace that the history of civilization is largely the history of weapons.

Puzzle #6

How one hates to think of oneself as alone. How one avoids it. It seems to imply rejection or unpopularity.

Puzzle #7

Make sure, as often as possible, you are doing something you'd be happy to die doing.

Puzzle #8

The world is full of magical things patiently waiting for our wits to grow sharper.

Puzzle #9

Patience, that blending of moral courage with physical timidity

Puzzle #10

My wallet is like an onion. Every time I open it, it makes me cry.

Puzzle #11

A diamond is just a lump of coal that did well under pressure.

Puzzle #12

I love being married. It's so great to find that one special person you want to annoy for the rest of your life.

Puzzle #13

I'm glad I don't have to hunt for my own food. I have no idea where sandwiches live.

Puzzle #14

Whatever you're doing, always give 100%. Unless you're donating blood

Puzzle #15

Don't worry. If Plan A doesn't work, there are 25 more letters in the alphabet.

Puzzle #16

I drink to make other people more interesting.

Puzzle #17

When you're in jail, a good friend will be trying to bail you out. A best friend will be in the cell next to you saying, 'Damn, that was fun.

Puzzle #18

My friends tell me I have an intimacy problem. But they don't really know me

Puzzle #19

The secret of staying young is to live honestly, eat slowly, and lie about your age.

Puzzle #20

Before you marry a person, you should first make them use a computer with slow Internet service to see who they really are.

Puzzle #21

I grew up with six brothers. That's how I learned to dance: waiting for the bathroom.

Puzzle #22

Never put off till tomorrow what you can do the day after tomorrow just as well.

Puzzle #23

Have you ever noticed that anybody driving slower than you is an idiot, and anyone going faster than you is a maniac?

Puzzle #24

A true optimist is the guy who falls off a skyscraper and after 50 floors thinks to himself – well, so far so good!

Puzzle #25

Alcohol does not solve any problems, but then again, neither does milk.

Puzzle #26

So be wise, because the world needs more wisdom, and if you cannot be wise, pretend to be someone who is wise, and then just behave like they would.

Puzzle #27

There is only one thing in the world worse than being talked about, and that is not being talked about.

Sudoku

Easy #1

3	1	6	2	4	8	7	5	9
2	5	9	3	7	1	4	6	8
4	8	7	9	5	6	3	2	1
1	3	2	4	6	9	5	8	7
7	6	8	5	1	2	9	3	4
9	4	5	8	3	7	6	1	2
5	7	1	6	2	4	8	9	3
8	2	3	7	9	5	1	4	6
6	9	4	1	8	3	2	7	5

Easy #2

8	2	9	1	6	3	5	4	7
7	5	4	2	9	8	3	1	6
3	6	1	7	4	5	2	9	8
2	8	5	4	7	1	9	6	3
1	3	7	6	8	9	4	5	2
4	9	6	3	5	2	7	8	1
5	4	3	8	2	6	1	7	9
9	1	8	5	3	7	6	2	4
6	7	2	9	1	4	8	3	5

Easy #3

2	4	8	7	1	6	5	3	9
3	5	7	2	9	8	6	4	1
6	9	1	3	5	4	7	2	8
1	3	6	5	4	9	8	7	2
7	2	9	6	8	3	1	5	4
4	8	5	1	2	7	9	6	3
5	6	4	9	3	1	2	8	7
8	1	2	4	7	5	3	9	6
9	7	3	8	6	2	4	1	5

Easy #4

2	6	4	3	1	5	9	8	7
5	3	7	8	2	9	1	6	4
1	8	9	6	7	4	3	2	5
6	5	2	1	9	3	7	4	8
7	4	1	5	8	6	2	3	9
3	9	8	7	4	2	5	1	6
9	2	5	4	3	8	6	7	1
4	7	6	2	5	1	8	9	3
8	1	3	9	6	7	4	5	2

Easy #5

8	2	5	7	6	1	9	3	4
7	1	6	9	4	3	5	2	8
4	9	3	8	2	5	1	6	7
3	4	7	6	9	2	8	1	5
2	5	1	4	3	8	6	7	9
6	8	9	5	1	7	2	4	3
5	7	2	3	8	6	4	9	1
1	3	4	2	5	9	7	8	6
9	6	8	1	7	4	3	5	2

Easy #6

3	2	7	4	5	9	6	1	8
6	5	9	3	1	8	4	2	7
8	1	4	2	6	7	5	9	3
2	6	5	9	8	4	7	3	1
7	4	8	6	3	1	2	5	9
9	3	1	5	7	2	8	4	6
5	9	6	7	2	3	1	8	4
1	7	3	8	4	5	9	6	2
4	8	2	1	9	6	3	7	5

Medium #1

9	1	3	8	2	7	6	4	5
6	2	7	5	3	4	1	8	9
8	5	4	1	9	6	2	3	7
2	9	6	4	5	1	8	7	3
1	4	8	2	7	3	5	9	6
3	7	5	9	6	8	4	2	1
4	8	9	3	1	5	7	6	2
7	3	1	6	8	2	9	5	4
5	6	2	7	4	9	3	1	8

Medium #2

1	3	7	2	8	6	4	5	9
2	9	6	5	3	4	8	7	1
8	4	5	9	1	7	6	2	3
4	1	8	6	2	9	7	3	5
6	2	9	3	7	5	1	8	4
7	5	3	1	4	8	9	6	2
3	7	2	8	9	1	5	4	6
9	6	4	7	5	3	2	1	8
5	8	1	4	6	2	3	9	7

Medium #3

6	3	2	1	7	8	5	9	4
8	9	1	3	4	5	6	2	7
5	4	7	6	2	9	1	8	3
7	2	5	9	3	1	4	6	8
3	6	9	2	8	4	7	5	1
4	1	8	5	6	7	9	3	2
2	5	4	8	1	6	3	7	9
1	8	6	7	9	3	2	4	5
9	7	3	4	5	2	8	1	6

Medium #4

5	1	7	2	4	8	6	9	3
2	9	3	6	1	7	4	5	8
6	8	4	5	3	9	2	1	7
4	3	6	9	8	1	5	7	2
7	5	1	4	6	2	8	3	9
9	2	8	7	3	5	1	4	6
1	6	2	7	5	3	9	8	4
8	7	9	1	2	4	3	6	5
3	4	5	8	9	6	7	2	1

Medium #5

3	1	9	4	5	7	6	2	8
4	2	5	8	6	1	9	7	3
6	8	7	9	3	2	5	1	4
7	6	3	2	1	5	4	8	9
8	4	2	3	9	6	1	5	7
5	9	1	7	8	4	2	3	6
1	5	4	6	7	3	8	9	2
2	3	8	1	4	9	7	6	5
9	7	6	5	2	8	3	4	1

Medium #6

2	7	3	1	5	8	4	6	9
8	1	9	3	6	4	2	7	5
4	6	5	2	9	7	3	8	1
6	9	7	5	2	3	8	1	4
3	4	8	7	1	9	5	2	6
1	5	2	4	8	6	9	3	7
5	3	4	6	7	2	1	9	8
9	2	6	8	4	1	7	5	3
7	8	1	9	3	5	6	4	2

Hard #1

9	1	2	6	3	5	8	4	7
3	5	6	4	8	7	1	2	9
4	8	7	1	9	2	5	3	6
8	4	3	9	1	6	5	7	2
1	6	5	2	7	3	9	8	4
7	2	9	5	4	8	6	1	3
5	7	4	8	6	9	2	3	1
2	9	1	3	5	4	7	6	8
6	3	8	7	2	1	4	9	5

Hard #2

5	2	1	9	4	3	7	6	8
6	8	9	2	5	7	1	3	4
3	4	7	1	8	6	9	5	2
1	3	8	5	7	2	4	9	6
7	5	4	8	6	9	2	1	3
2	9	6	4	3	1	5	8	7
4	1	3	7	9	8	6	2	5
8	7	2	6	1	5	3	4	9
9	6	5	3	2	4	8	7	1

Hard #3

4	8	5	2	7	3	9	1	6
9	7	1	5	6	4	2	8	3
2	6	3	9	1	8	7	4	5
6	4	2	8	3	1	5	9	7
5	3	8	4	9	7	1	6	2
1	9	7	6	5	2	8	3	4
7	2	4	1	8	6	3	5	9
3	1	6	7	5	9	4	2	8
8	5	9	3	4	2	6	7	1

Hard #4

4	1	3	7	2	8	6	5	9
2	9	6	1	4	5	8	3	7
8	7	5	3	6	9	4	2	1
3	5	9	2	1	4	7	6	8
7	2	4	8	5	6	1	9	3
6	8	1	9	3	7	2	4	5
9	3	2	6	8	1	5	7	4
5	6	8	4	7	3	9	1	2
1	4	7	5	9	2	3	8	6

Hard #5	Hard #6	Hard #7	Hard #8

6	5	2	4	3	1	7	8	9
3	1	9	7	8	2	5	4	6
4	8	7	6	5	9	3	2	1
1	4	5	2	6	8	9	3	7
9	7	6	1	4	3	8	5	2
8	2	3	5	9	7	1	6	4
5	9	4	3	1	6	2	7	8
2	3	8	9	7	4	6	1	5
7	6	1	8	2	5	4	9	3

7	9	2	5	1	8	6	4	3
5	1	3	7	4	6	9	2	8
8	4	6	3	2	9	1	7	5
1	2	4	6	3	7	8	5	9
3	6	5	8	9	2	7	1	4
9	8	7	1	5	4	3	6	2
2	3	8	4	6	1	5	9	7
6	5	9	2	7	3	4	8	1
4	7	1	9	8	5	2	3	6

2	3	1	7	9	6	5	8	4
4	8	6	3	1	5	7	2	9
9	7	5	4	8	2	6	3	1
7	4	8	1	6	3	2	9	5
3	6	9	5	2	7	4	1	8
1	5	2	9	4	8	3	7	6
6	9	4	2	7	1	8	5	3
8	2	3	6	5	9	1	4	7
5	1	7	8	3	4	9	6	2

2	6	4	9	7	3	8	5	1
8	9	3	5	2	1	6	4	7
5	1	7	6	8	4	2	9	3
3	5	6	8	9	7	4	1	2
1	8	9	3	4	2	5	7	6
4	7	2	1	6	5	3	8	9
9	2	1	4	3	8	7	6	5
6	3	8	7	5	9	1	2	4
7	4	5	2	1	6	9	3	8

Trivia Quizzes

1. A) Corn, beans, and squash
2. A) 206
3. B) Bourbon, Campari, and sweet vermouth
4. B) Michelangelo
5. B) 3
6. A) Hippocrates
7. A) Venus
8. B) 5
9. B) 2007
10. B) 1989
11. A) Au
12. B) Minnesota
13. B) 60 feet, 6 inches
14. A) Jean-Paul Sartre
15. B) Bangers and mash
16. A) He was a copper miner
17. C) The USS Constitution
18. A) Navy
19. C) Hydrogen
20. B) Benjamin Franklin
21. B) Alaska
22. A) Some Like It Hot
23. A) Chocolate, vanilla, and strawberry
24. B) Crusader Rabbit
25. A) Life cereal
26. A) Some Pig
27. B) Coca Cola
28. C) Vermouth
29. C) Wendy's
30. A) Great Dane
31. B) Citrus
32. B) Spanish moss
33. B) Redwood National Park
34. A) Solid, liquid, gas
35. C) Parentheses
36. B) California
37. A) Italy
38. B) Double dribble
39. A) Delta
40. B) Photosynthesis
41. B) Andes

42. C) Erosion
43. B) Nitrogen
44. B) Unicorn
45. B) Komodo Dragon
46. B) John Adams
47. B) Margaret Thatcher
48. C) Choux
49. B) Bavarian Motor Works
50. A) Ouzo

Labyrinths

Maze #1

Maze #2

Maze #3

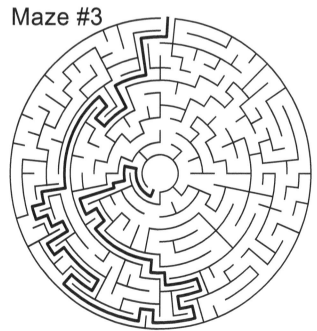

Maze #4

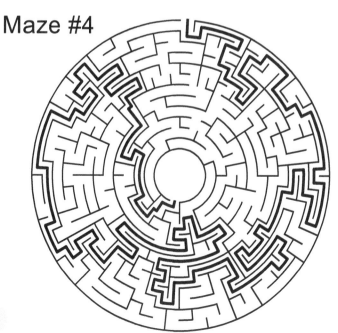

Maze #5

Maze #6

Maze #7

Maze #8

Maze #9

Maze #10

Maze #11

Maze #12

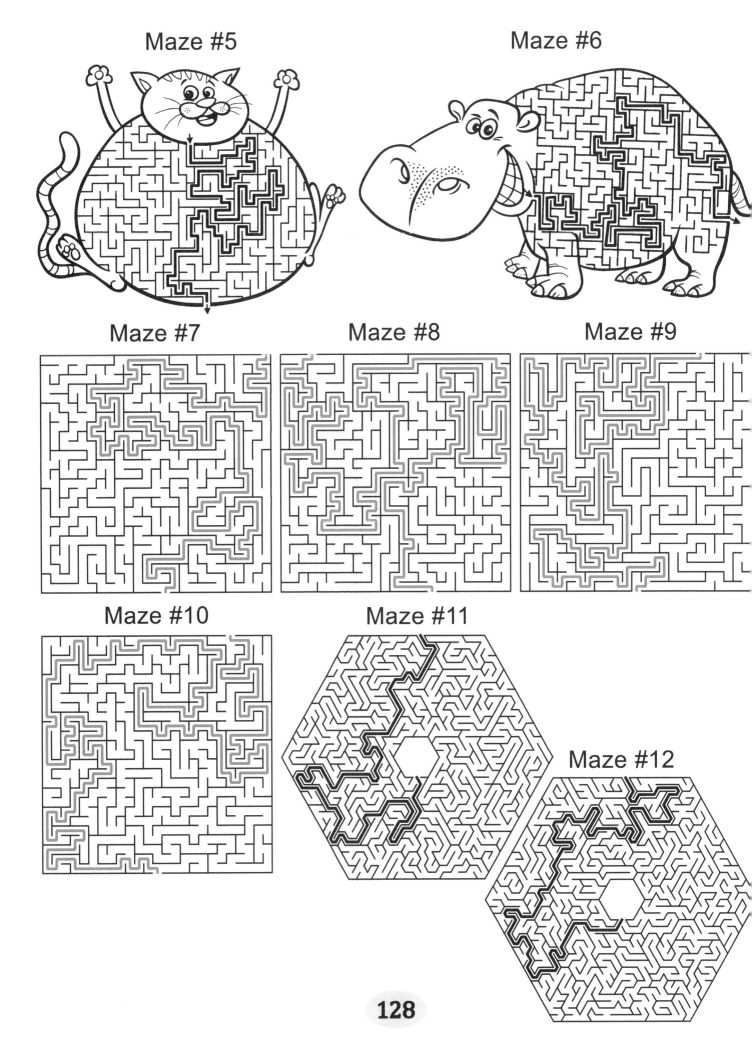

Maze #13

Maze #14

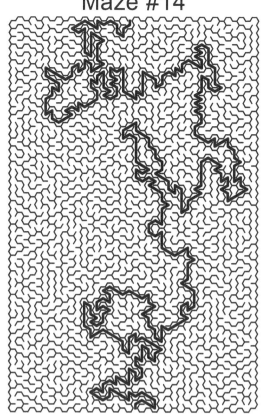

Maze #15

Maze #16

129

Word Fill-In Puzzles

Puzzle #1

Puzzle #2

Puzzle #3

Puzzle #4

Puzzle #5

Puzzle #6

Puzzle #7

Puzzle #8

Puzzle #9

Puzzle #10

Made in United States
Troutdale, OR
12/06/2024

25926656R00073